CHEERS!

RED / LIGHTNING BOOKS

CHEERS!

AROUND THE WORLD IN 80 TOASTS

BRANDON COOK

This book is a publication of

Red Lightning Books
1320 East 10th Street
Bloomington, Indiana 47405 USA

redlightningbooks.com

Manufactured in Canada

Cataloging information is available from
the Library of Congress.

ISBN 978-1-68435-145-9 (hardback)
ISBN 978-1-68435-147-3 (ebook)

First Printing 2021

For my Mom and Dad

CONTENTS

Foreword   ix
Acknowledgments   xiii

PART ONE. EUROPE

1. Albanian   2
2. Basque (Euskara)   6
3. Breton   10
4. Bulgarian   14
5. Croatian   18
6. Czech   22
7. Dutch   26
8. English   30
9. Estonian   36
10. Finnish   40
11. French   44
12. Galician   50
13. German   54
14. Greek   60
15. Hungarian   64
16. Irish   68
17. Italian   72

18. Latvian   76
19. Lithuanian   80
20. Maltese   84
21. Norwegian   88
22. Polish   92
23. Portuguese   96
24. Romanian   100
25. Russian   104
26. Serbian   108
27. Slovak   112
28. Slovenian   116
29. Spanish   120
30. Swedish   124
31. Turkish   128
32. Ukrainian   132
33. Welsh   136

PART TWO. EURASIA
34. Armenian   142
35. Azerbaijani   146
36. Belarusian   150
37. Georgian   154
38. Kazakh   158
39. Mongolian   162
40. Tajik   166
41. Uzbek   172

PART THREE. ASIA & AUSTRONESIA
42. Burmese (Myanmar)   178
43. Cebuano   182
44. Chinese (Mandarin)   186
45. Chinese (Dialects)   190
46. Hawaiian   194
47. Hindi   198
48. Indonesian   202
49. Japanese   206
50. Khmer   212
51. Korean   216
52. Malayalam   220
53. Malay   224

54. Nepali   228
55. Sinhala   232
56. Tagalog   236
57. Tamil   240
58. Thai   244
59. Vietnamese   248

PART FOUR. AFRICA & THE MIDDLE EAST
60. Afrikaans   254
61. Amharic   258
62. Arabic   262
63. Hausa   268
64. Igbo   272
65. Kinyarwanda   276
66. Persian (Farsi)   280
67. Somali   286
68. Swahili   290
69. Wolof   294
70. Xhosa   298
71. Yoruba   302

PART FIVE. ANCIENT, CONSTRUCTED, AND MISCELLANEOUS

72. American Sign Language (ASL)   308

73. Ancient Greek   312

74. Aramaic (Syriac)   318

75. Esperanto   324

76. Hebrew   328

77. Latin   332

78. Na'vi   338

79. Quenya (Elvish)   342

80. Toki Pona   348

Language List by Country   353

Bibliography   359

FOREWORD

For a significant amount of time that people have been drinking, they have been toasting. Unfortunately, no one knows with any certainty for how long. Unlike the origins of alcohol, which can be more or less confidently dated based on the analysis of fermented fruit, it is considerably more difficult uncovering the origins of toasts. How do you date a clink, a glance, a word?

Short answer: you don't. What we do know is that since at least as far back as the ancient world, people have been raising glasses to their comrades. Achilles drinks to Patroclus in the *Iliad*, and even earlier than that, in ancient Egypt, drunkenness via beer or wine was central to many religious festivals. If ever we discover the origins of this marriage between drinking and celebration, we will find the beginnings of toasting.

It's likely that you're familiar with some of the stories behind the tradition of clinking glasses. One of the most popular goes that in an ancient time of feuding warlords, paranoia of being poisoned was so great that goblets were ritualistically smashed together so that the alcohol would fly and mix into the other cups. Another story goes that wine glasses in medieval Europe were delicately clinked in order to imitate the sound of church bells. Unfriendly devils and demons lurking about would then scuttle off in fear of the Christian piety. Still another story says that toasting started as a ritual to invoke all five senses—the smell, taste, and sight of the wine; the touch and sound of the glass. Delightful as these stories are, that is precisely what they are—stories.

This book isn't concerned with discussing toasting as ancient history or even with the story of how it became the global phenomenon it is today. It's more of a guidebook exploring how more than eighty languages express the word and culture of our English "cheers." I don't mean to suggest that every country in the world has the same culture and custom of toasting as in those countries where English is the native language. Rather, the toasts provided in this book take on a variety of forms and meanings. Readers will find that in Burmese, the word for "cheers" means something like "let's hit it," reminiscent of a general leading his army into battle. The Somali toast isn't used as a prelude to alcohol but for drinking camel milk. Aramaic gives a word meaning "love"; Hausa, a phrase meaning "rejoice in your heart." The Na'vi language, of the 2009 film *Avatar*, has a toast although its humanoid speakers lack glasses, and Quenya, J. R. R. Tolkien's Elvish language, has both a toast and drinks to toast with, though you probably can't find them in any liquor store.

More than its connection with alcohol, this book celebrates toasting and its connection with language. Americans and foreign languages have a sticky relationship at best. Many of us still have memories of frivolous high school French or Latin courses where a great deal of instruction seemed to leave us equipped with no more than the phrase "I want to use the bathroom" and some useful curse words. The remedy for the United

States' difficult relationship to languages probably won't be found here (though you never know); however, at the very least it's worthwhile to look at language as the wonderful and interesting phenomenon it is. The texts below the word and pronunciation of "cheers" are meant to act as a kind of highlight reel showcasing language's more bizarre and interesting aspects.

Finally, a book about toasting would do itself a disservice if it didn't include some information about drinks. The "Tasting Notes" list a few of that region's more popular beverages, alcoholic and nonalcoholic. These lists are far from exhaustive, and travelers with serious interests in the local brews would be wise to consult more specialized guidebooks, dialogue with the locals, or both.

Cheers! is a guidebook for language and culture. Its intention is to make world cultures more accessible and languages more fun. My hope is you'll flip to any language that catches your fancy and discover something new and interesting, but if you come away with no more than a few more strange words pottering around your head, I'll count that a victory. Cheers!

ACKNOWLEDGMENTS

Whenever possible, I have drawn from personal experience and knowledge. As I do not have in-depth knowledge of all eighty of the languages represented, I am extremely grateful for the hundreds of speakers on iTalki and HiNative who graciously responded to my queries and assisted with the proofreading and editing processes. I've tried to give credit to everyone who has helped me in this process—my apologies if I have overlooked you:

(Albanian) Edlira D; (Armenian) Armine; (Azerbaijani) Zemfira; (Basque) Xubixaretta Ibai; (Breton) Professor Kevin Rottet; (Bulgarian) Nicola Chushkov, Violeta Argelova, Martin Christov; (Croatian) Suzana Anđelkovic, Sreten W.; (Czech) Jan Tatousek, Martin Meidl; (Dutch) Sonia Azamifard, Kal van Stigt; (Estonian) Heli Aomets; (Finnish) Jaako; (French) Maud Thamié Lopez; (Galician) Martín Redonda Fernández, Miguel Caamaño; (Georgian) Giorgi Lotsulashvili, Anna Sanikidze, Dewy Peters, Keti; (Greek) Constantinos Soteriou; (Hungarian) Peter; (Irish) Coligno; (Italian) Giulia; (Kazakh) Merein, Ansar Sarkytov; (Latvian) Krists; (Lithuanian) Šarunas Zavadskas; (Maltese) Andre Xerri, Loron Grixti; (Mongolian) Adiyasuren; (Polish) Tomasz Suchaja; (Portuguese) Camila Alvers, Tawanne Siqueira; (Romanian) Ovidiu Nicolas, Andrei

Victor; (Russian) Polina; (Serbian) Suzana Anđelkovic, Nash Antic; (Slovak) Sylvia Vitekova, Michal Michalik; (Spanish) Jaime Rivera; (Swedish) Mahyar Hemmati, Matthias Lindström, Albin Einarson; (Turkish) Keely Bakken; (Ukrainian) Olga Rezniko; (Welsh) Jonathan Mills, Professor Kevin Rottet; (Burmese) Kenneth Wong, Jar Puu, Cherry P.W., Min Khaung; (Cebuano) Caomhin, Neciforo Pesiao Jr., Kevin Marc; (Chinese) ChenCen, Shimin Qin; (Hawaiian) Professor Puakea Nogelmeier; (Hindi) Priyam; (Indonesian) Rio Wibowo, Yoga; (Khmer) Yulong Vy, Limit; (Korean) John YoHan Park; (Malayalam) Antony; (Malaysian) Jeffrey Biyud; (Nepali) Sunil Rajbahak, Saugat, Samrat Uphadyay; (Sinhalese) Shamil; (Tagalog) Joanna Abaya, Brylle Jansen Llaguno; (Tamil) Arun; (Thai) Sakornpob Nithisopa; (Vietnamese) Phạm Thị Xuân Mai, Lan Anh Phan, Hoang Kha; (Afrikaans) Richard du Plessis, Annelie van der Merwe, Christelle Lotter; (Amharic) Pheruz; (Arabic) Hassaine Daouadji Mohammed Amin, Omar Kamal; (Persian) Raena Mazahernasab, Professor Shahyar Daneshgar, Mahdi Birjandi; (Hausa) Mashaer; (Igbo) Sapphire Agwu; (Kinyarwanda) Erin Baumgartel; (Somali) A. Jama; (Swahili) Professor Richard Mathias Nyamahanga; (Somali) Aisha Moha; (Tajik) Maruf Ibragimov; (Uzbek) Alisher; (Wolof) Mame Anna Fall; (Xhosa) Luvo; (Yoruba) Tayo Ayinde, Professor Matthew Ajibade; (Ancient Greek) Michela, Oscar Goldman, Pantazis Stougianas; (American Sign Language) Aunt Mary Betts; (Aramaic) Emarceen; (Esperanto) Thomas Alexander, Martin LeLarge; (Hebrew) Elena Luchina, Sam Sternfeld, Ita; (Latin) Ivana Ciric; (Na'vi) Learn Na'vi Community; (Quenya) Council of Elrond.

Much of the information in this book has come from combing through articles on the internet. Travel websites and YouTube have been particularly helpful in putting the texts together. I am indebted to the channels sweetandtastyTV for the information about Korean and to StreetEnglishTV for Japanese.

Huge thank yous to Blakely Meyer, Preston, and Shimin for their devoted readings and re-readings.

Lastly, my thanks to everybody at Red Lightning for making the publication process such smooth sailing, and for producing such a beautiful book.

PART ONE

EUROPE

1

ALBANIAN

"Gëzuar"
(he zoo'ar)

("Happy")

Albania is smack dab
in the center of wine territory.
In fact, the land has been home
to the grape for between 4,000 and
6,000 years—a substantial history,
although not quite as ancient as that
belonging to the regions of modern
Greece and Georgia, where grapes
have been cultivated for
over 8,500 years.

The name Albanoi crops up around the year AD 1080. The name stuck in more places than one: some linguists believe that the root *alb*, meaning "mountain" or "hill," later found its way to mainland Europe, where it became "alp." Traveling still further, it's tempting to conclude the root morphed into the Albion of pre-seventeenth-century Great Britain. However, it's more likely that the Albion connection came from the Proto-Indo-European root *albho*, meaning "white," and the same root responsible for this collection of sprightly English words: *dauben*, *auburn*, *elven*, *abele* (white poplar), *albedo* (reflected luster), *albescent* (becoming white), *Alba* (Scotland), *albatross*, and *albino* (of course). "Elf" and "alf" also appear in this cast of Tolkien characters—Elfhelm, Elfstan, Elfstone, Elfwine, and Gandalf—and remnants of the root are also found in the name Oberon, the fairy king of Shakespeare's *A Midsummer Night's Dream*. Are the two *albs* from the same source? It'd be tempting to say yes—English doesn't yet have any Albanian influence, and I, for one, think it's high time for some.

During its early history, Albanian split off from the rest of the Indo-European languages and made its own family, of which it remains the sole survivor. Hence, it doesn't sound like or resemble any other European language. Just take a look at some of its fantastic words, like

mbyllizogojen ("may God close his mouth"), meaning "wolf," and *shtozovalle* ("may God increase their round dances"), for "fairy."

Fortunately, the Albanian toast, *gëzuar* ("happy," "merry"), is easier to wrap your tongue around than wolves and fairies. It is said after each drink and accompanied with a clink. And as for beverages, fermented raki is drunk about as often as wine, although during the five hundred years of sober Ottomans and forty years of communist collectivization, wine of the time was limited to exactly two, a red and a white.

But viticulture is staging a comeback. Since collectivization ended in 1991, there are now more than thirty wineries working with the dozen native grapes to produce new and innovative wines, about five million bottles a year in a country of three million people. For a good sampling, consider a chilled Shesh i Bardhë ("White Field") or aged Shesh i Zi ("Black Field"), both traditional Albanian varieties grown at Çobo Winery, whose vineyards are overseen by the incredible Mount Shpirag. It's certainly worth a toast, if not a visit.

TASTING NOTE
Skrapari raki and plum raki before or after meals; coffee, Italian or Turkish style.

BASQUE

(Euskara)

"Topaketa"
(topa keta)

("Cheers")

If there's one European language that can be said to have cracked the tidy Indo-European language bowl, that would be Basque. Coming across this language isolate on the European continent, where the relations between languages are all more or less clear, is a bit like panning for gold and accidentally discovering the bones of a dinosaur.

You can't say how or when it got there, but what you do know is that what you're looking at is unlike anything you've ever seen.

Basque Country (Euskal Herria) is on the western end of the Pyrenees in tourist country, north-central Spain and southwestern France. You can throw whatever you want at Basque—Carthaginians, Gauls, proto-Celts, Visigoths, a Roman Empire—and you're not going to change it.

Its origins are mysteries laced with intrigue. Hypotheses are as colorful as you can imagine and come in whatever form you prefer, like Starbursts. There are some linking Basques with the Saharan Berber tribes, with proto-Celts, with the trans-Caucasians . . . and with Martians. The celebrated Basque scholar Koldo Mitxelen remarked that the real mystery of the Basque language is not its mysterious origins but its continued survival. Which is to say, the facts of Basque's history that linguists across the board are dead sure about amount to ‾_(ツ)_/‾.

What scholars *do* know is that the language descends from one of the Pre-Indo-European languages spoken on the continent roughly five thousand years ago and that it segregated itself in the stronghold of the Pyrenees while its neighbors were either killed off or absorbed into the various empires mentioned above. After a long period of solitude, Basque emerged to discover itself a language island with some French- and Spanish-inspired dialects.

Basque culture is colorful and lively, occasionally drunk, and full of festivals. *Topa* ("toast"), sometimes *topaketa*, is the go-to word for any occasion, whether with a cool Spanish beer, such as Pagoa or Keler, or a chilled cup of *patxaran*—that most Basque of beverages: a reddish liquor distilled from wild sloes. Notable mentions to the lexicon also include the more formal *guregatik* (*goo ree gat ik*, meaning "for us") and the rarer *osasuna* (*o'sa'soon'a*, meaning "health"). Nothing fancy required for toasting—just make sure to include everyone when clinking glasses.

3

BRETON

"Yec'hed mat"
(yih'hid mat)

("Good health")

Who wants to settle on the words "good health" when you can wish your buddy "joy to your throat" (*joe d'ho kargouilhenn*)! Why say "forty-five" if you can say "five and two twenties," or say "seventy-seven" instead of "seventeen and three twenties"?

11

Happy throats and numerical increments of twenty are both aspects of Breton, the Celtic language spoken sporadically throughout Brittany, in northwest France.

Toasts are popular in Brittany, and to make sure you get the most out of your drink, you should be prepared to dispense with plenty of "good health" (*yih'hid mat*) and plenty of blessings. "Bennozh deoc'h ha yec'hedoù!" is a nice one, meaning "A blessing to you and to health." And there is also the more poetic "Yec'hed mad deomp toud, hemañ zo o vont en roud!"—"Good health to all of us, this drink on its way!" A nicer way of saying "Down the hatch" I've yet to hear.

Despite the widespread use of French, Breton has a resilient group of speakers estimated at around 200,000—about a quarter of the speakers of its relative Welsh. Alas, heroic resilience in the face of stupendous odds (English and French) is something too often demanded from the Celtic languages. Breton's close cousin Cornish (in Cornwall, Southwest England) and more distant cousin Manx (on the Isle of Man)—lacking the momentum of the revival campaigns that gave Irish and Scottish Gaelic their second winds— stand at death's gate with only about 2,500 speakers between the two of them. Fortunately, momentum for Breton doesn't show signs of slowing.

If you find yourself in Brittany, try to show some Breton love while also sampling some of the popular wines. Naturally, these are plentiful in France, but travelers may also want to try the popular Kir Breton: a cider and black currant aperitif traditionally served in a ceramic bowl. Or if ciders aren't your thing, perhaps a glass of *chouchen*—an aperitif brewed with a combination of cider and honey. It looks like a sunset in a glass. Throat blessings, Kir, and chouchen aside, Breton's other contribution to world culture is the word *bijou*, now seen in French as the term for "jewelry." English has also adopted (via French) the term *menhir* for the upright standing stone monument lifted in prehistoric times, but neither word will get you as far or buy you as much love as "Yec'hed mat."

4

BULGARIAN

"Наздраве"
(nazdrav'ay)

("To health")

Contending for the title of world's oldest wino, here's Bulgaria weighing in at 4000 BC, which is right on par with Armenia but a few millennia behind Georgia, Azerbaijan, and Iran.

Bulgarians talk about the history of their grape with justifiable pride. Justifiable owing to its longevity as well as its fame. Pliny the Elder calls Thracian (Bulgarian) wines the oldest in the world, and Homer writes of a celebration between Odysseus and a priest, Maro, who hands over "twelve amphorae sweet, undiluted wine, divine drink." So divine in fact that the priest then goes on to "mix it with twenty times as much water."

Twenty times is maybe an exaggeration, but the dilution would have been necessary in ancient times. Even today, some wine drinkers recommend adding a splash of water to the glass to enhance flavors and pronunciation. While the technique may still be in place, modern wines differ substantially from those of the ancients or the medievals, which weren't so much wines as thick, spiced, vinegary, heavily fortified stews.

Bulgarian wine lays claim to longevity, literary prestige, and the fact that during the Soviet era, Bulgaria became the fourth largest wine producer in the world. After the fall of the Soviet Union and the loss of its most supportive buyer, things went south for Bulgarian wine, but the vineyards have been hard at work regaining their former glory. As of 2016, there are a reported 148,000 acres of vineyards spread over 262 producers in the five wine regions.

TASTING NOTE
rakia, Kamenitza
beer, local wines.

What kind of wine? There's a little bit of everything. Merlot and cabernet sauvignon account for roughly half. Local grapes include *mavrud* and "early *melnik*." But we ought to be clear that wine isn't all there is. As in most eastern European countries, you can also get *rakia* (fruit brandy), considered by many to be the national beverage. And it would be negligent of me not to also mention *ar'yan*, a chilled yogurt and salt drink originally from Turkey, sometimes called *laban*.

Bulgarian is Slavic and shares the Slavic toast *na zdrave* (to health). Keep your eyes locked to your host's to show your thanks and courtesy when sampling any one of Bulgaria's hundreds of different types of wine. For a bit more cultural flavor, you can also consider sharing this bit of Bulgarian coaching: "I da padnem, I da biem, pak shte se napiem" ("Win or lose, we still booze"). Isn't that the spirit!

5

CROATIAN

"Živjeli,"
"U zdravlje"
(zheev ye lee),
(oo zdrav'lee)

("Cheers,"
"To health")

A golden rule of Balkan toasts: if you've heard one "Zhiveli," you've heard them all. Croatians express their version of the staple Balkan toast with a different vowel sound as the middle syllable—zhiv*y*eli rather than zhiv*ee*li.

Croatians will also say "U zdravlje," as well as "Živjeli," but that's about it. But what could possibly account for this astonishing coincidence in živjelis?

Once upon a time in the early nineteenth century, a Serbian folklorist named Vuk Karadžić got the idea to simplify his native Serbian by introducing a simplified Cyrillic alphabet. Simplification in the name of standardization was a theme later taken up by the Croatian poet Ljudevit Gaj, who urged his countrymen to adopt as a literary standard a dialect spoken throughout the Balkans called Shtokavian. (*Shto* means "what," so the name of the dialect literally translates into something like "whatese.") The suggestion was debated, bandied about, tossed around, laid aside, taken back up, and finally, by the end of the nineteenth century, accepted as a pretty good idea. The result was later called Serbo-Croatian or Croato-Serbian—a rather testy balance, like Lennon-McCartney. Later, this stylistic cobbling encompassed even more languages and became the eloquently termed Bosnian-Croatian-Montenegrin-Serbian, or BCMS. By 2009, the former Yugoslavia was a puzzle board of newly and seminewly independent countries, and a national language was a patriotic hammer in the toolbox of independence. BCMS lost its hyphens as Bosnians claimed a Bosnian language, Serbians Serbian, Croatians Croatian, and Montenegrins Montenegrin. The separation is mostly political, but there is a difference in the alphabet. Serbians use the Cyrillic and Latin, Bosnians Latin, Montenegrins nominally both but leaning toward Latin, and Croatians strictly Latin. This might not seem like much of a difference, but take a moment to reflect on how the extra *l* in *traveller* or the *s* in *organise* immediately distinguishes a Brit from an American.

Now as for drinks, the go-to liquor of Eastern Europe is rakia/*rakija* in all its forms (cherry, pear, plum, walnut, etc.). Too many shots and even the most resilient drinker may have trouble getting out of bed in the morning, but if you're lucky, before bed your Croatian comrades will prescribe you a good dose of sage tea—Croatia's hangover remedy. In addition to some of the bluest beaches on the planet, Croatia has also got a flourishing wine market. While in Croatia, take some time to sample the dark red *plavac mali* (considered a relative of zinfandel), white *pošip*, or the dessert wine *prošek* (no relation to prosecco).

If you're eating out, ask for a recommendation and you'll get something new every night. And while you're at it, why not supplement your language learning with the Serbo-Croatian/BCMS or just plain Croatian version of *bon appetit*: "Dobar tek."

TASTING NOTE
rakia, *šljivovica* fruit brandy, Karlovačko, Ožujsko, and Pan beers.

6

CZECH

"Na zdraví" *(na zdrav'ee)*

("To health")

When it comes to Slavic tongues, there are some unfortunate generalizations people tend to make. If languages were cars, Romance is your high-end sports, Germanic is a jeep, and Slavic is a tank. Tough to handle, it can take years of practice to get to a point where you finally feel comfortable enough to take it out for a spin. Slavic language learners will inevitably complain about the many consonant clusters.

Clunky vowels. The impossible grammar. One of the worst you can make is to tell a Slavic-language speaker that her language *sounds* like a language it's not. Asking a Polish or a Czech speaker if the language she's speaking is Russian might get you a slap in the face.

The longer you spend with Slavic languages, the more you'll discover how unique and beautiful they are, though they do share many similarities. Bulgarian, Polish, Czech, Slovak, and Russian have all got the same toast ("to your health"), and the toasts do sound alike. Alike, yes, but not the same. Take the Russian word for "to work," *работать*. Czechs Latinized it into *rabotat* and colloquialized it into a term meaning "drudgery." The word then got fed into English via the work of the Czech sci-fi writer Karel Čapek as *robot*, and thus English gained a new and popular addition.

Now take *na zdravi*. Czech has an "ee" sound at the end, instead of the Russian "ye." Czech drinkers also don't give the marathon toasts favored by Russians, and it is acceptable to simply leave it at *na zdravi* without embellishment. If you want to add more, say *na* (meaning "to") plus whatever it is you're honoring: "to our business" is *na náš obchod* (*nash ob'hod*), and "to us" is *na nás*. "Lots of luck" will be *hodně štěstí* (*hodnye shtyesti*), and *hodně štěstí, zdraví a spokojenosti* is a very handsome toast to "good luck, good health, and well-being."

How do you take your toasts? Probably with a good brew. Czechs have been making beer for over a thousand years—the tradition has its roots in the Benedictine Břevnov Monastery, which continues to make beer to this day. The Czech Republic also holds the highest consumption per capita in the world, outpacing Germany. Staropramen, Pilsner Urquell, and Budwar are some of the more famous exported brews, but really if you ask a Czech, he or she will either glorify Pilsner and lambast Staropramen, or vice versa.

Before you really get going, however, there are a few safety tips to remember: look your toastee eye to eye, and do not cross arms. Although no one will tell you exactly *why*, doing so will entail dire consequences for your sex life.

TASTING NOTE
Pilsner Urquell, Staropramen, Velkopopovický Kozel beers; šljivovica fruit brandy, Becherovka liqueur.

7

DUTCH

"Proost"
(proast)
("Cheers")

The Netherlands as a colonial power is a country of lost opportunities. Let's go back to the year 1620. Indonesia, Sumatra, Java, Malaysia, Taiwan, and Japan have been seeing the Dutch East India Company—the Vereenigde Oost-Indische Compagnie—flag for years. Cape Towners wish each other *Goede dag*.

Amsterdam enjoys a monopoly on trade with Japan in Dejima, and New York is Nieuw-Nederland. Flash forward to the year 1850. Dejima is still there, but it'll only last another five years. South African *Goede dag* now sounds like "Goeie." And all those outposts in the Far East? What's the legacy of three hundred years of trade in Malaysia, Taiwan, Indonesia? Apart from some mangled Malay (which became the basis for the Bahasa Indonesian still spoken today) and an outpost in Batavia, not much.

However, if you're willing to make a bit of a stretch, you could argue that the Dutch language (or rather a language very close to it) very nearly missed out on tremendous global success. If you're in the Netherlands, walk north about 150 kilometers from Amsterdam, and you'll be in Friesland, home of Frisian. The closest relative to English, Frisian is separated from its brother by about two hundred miles. This was the distance it had to cross when, in the fifth century (a time of much migration if you're a Germanic tribe), it dumped itself into the Anglo-Saxon melting pot, where it mixed and developed freely with Old English. The two languages would have been mutually intelligible for a while, possibly up until the Norman invasion of England in 1066. However, after this, English Anglo-Saxon, loaded with Latin, Welsh syntax, and an army of new French loan words, would have resembled an entirely different beast compared to Frisian, which ultimately returned home to its coastal Friesland to soak up some of the regional Dutch. Frisian is there still, the estranged Old English brother of some 800,000 speakers. How much English owes to the Frisian influence or vice versa no one can say for certain, but it is tempting to imagine what the language might look like today had it only picked up a little more Latin or French.

TASTING NOTE
Amstel, Heineken, regional beers, Bols *jenever* gin.

We English speakers have inherited the French "cheers" and not the Dutch, which looks like *proost* but is pronounced "proast," the same as the German. And, like the Germans, natives will caution you that a *proost* spoken without looking eye to eye will result in seven years' bad sex. The superstition is commonplace in Europe, and travelers would be wise, as in driving, to keep eyes locked firmly ahead at all times.

The Dutch beers Heineken and Amstel are known the world over; if you're in the mood to sample something different, you'll have to find a worthy substitute, such as Hettog Jan or Jupiler. Luckily, in Amsterdam microbreweries alone produce over two thousand different brews and *speciaalbier*. Amsterdam is also home to the beer supermarket De Bierkoning, where even the most exotic beer tastes can be satisfied. The Bierkonig is truly the toast of Dutch culture—I mean, along with those guys Rembrandt and Vermeer and van Gogh.

As for toasting, if the simple *proost* isn't enough, you can try proosting to something specific (birthday, promotion, graduation, etc.) or proosting *op je gezondheid* (to good health).

8

ENGLISH

"Cheers"
(cheers)

The busie Sun (and one would guess
By's drunken fiery face no less)
Drinks up the Sea, and when h'as done,
The Moon and Stars drink up the Sun.
They drink and dance by their own light,
They drink and revel all the night.

Nothing in Nature's Sober found,
But an eternal Health goes round.
Fill up the Bowl then, fill it high,
Fill all the Glasses there, for why
Should every creature drink but I,
Why, Man of Morals, tell me why?

—ABRAHAM COWLEY, "Drinking"

31

What's in a toast? That which we call a cheers, by any other name, would sound as sweet? Well, if this book says one thing and one thing only, it is that all toasts certainly do *not* sound the same across the board. Hell, even the *English* toasts have their differences. Chug! Down the hatch! Bottoms up! Of course, we all share "cheers"—this from a term in Old French, the language that seeped into England following William the Conqueror's victory in 1066. However, Anglo-Saxon had been enjoying its own toast well before the French language got involved.

Go back as far as the twelfth century, and you can find the lovely An-glo-Saxon word *wassail*, a mishmash of the phrase *Wæs þu hæl* (*was thoo hal*: "Be you in good health!"), a greeting used during medieval Christ-mastime when the Anglo-Saxons imbibed from a communal bowl of hot mulled cider: the wassailing bowl. The proper response when someone wishes you "Good hæl" is "Drinc hæl!" And drink those wassailers have done right up to our modern day. There's even a catchy wassailing song from English rock band Blur.

But you can't drink hot wine the whole year round, and Great Britain (and, later, the United States) has had enormously varied experiences with its alcohol. Shakespeare's plays swim in oceans of booze. Booze as character: the fat knight John Falstaff declares that if he had a thou-sand sons, "the first human principle I would teach them should be to forswear thin potations and to addict themselves to sack"—sack being Spanish sherry. Booze as plot device: Richard III's brother Clarence is drowned in a giant cask of Malmsey wine. And booze as proverb: leav-ing aside Sir John and Sir Toby Belch, there is this from Autolycus, in

"The Winter's Tale": "A quart of ale is a dish for a king." Ale—patriotic ale, according to Andrew Boorde's popular sixteenth-century "Dyetary of Health" was "for the English man a natural drink," and was also the Bard's own choice, as opposed to beer, "a natural drink for a Dutch man," even though Elizabethan England was a great connoisseur of beer, sporting such luminous, vaguely craft beer titles as Huffecap, Mad Dog, Father Woresonne, Angels's Food, and Dragon's Milk.

Beer and ale eventually gave way to champagne, whose bubbles were as much a cause of delight then as now. Champagne was the favorite beverage of many luminaries, not least of which was Ben Franklin, for whom drinking and drunkenness were cause of much fascination. In 1736, under the name Silence Dogood, he even published a list of two hundred synonyms for the word *inebriated*. "They are seldom known to be drunk," writes Dogood, "though they are very often boozey, cogey, tipsey, fox'd, merry, mellow, fuddl'd, groatable, confoundedly cut, see two moons, are among the philistines, in a very good humor, see the sun, or the sun has shone upon them; they clip the King's English, are almost froze, feavourish, in their Altitude, Pretty well entered," and so on. We can also add to this *gannontinouaratonseri*, the word for "completely inebriated" in one of the Native American languages spoken around New England, and *beordruncen*, our Anglo-Saxon term for "drunk."

Alas, none of these colorful words has caught on in either New Zealand or Australia, although luckily "cheers" has made it down to that continent, plus some local inflection. Australian "Cheers, mate" is pronounced "Cheese mite." If you feel like sparring, you can also say: "Cheers, big

ears," and the retort: "Same goes, big nose." New Zealand Kiwis raise a glass with neither a cheers nor a cheese but a "Churs," as in "Churs, bro," and then it's down the hatch.

From Latin *prosit* to Anglo-Saxon *wassail* to Old French *chier* to English "cheers": What does the future have in store for drinking's most beloved word? Maybe taking a hint from Asia, "bottoms up" will take its place; however, I think not. If I had to put my money on any true contender to the spirit, culture, and arbitrariness of cheers, I'd put it on "Dilly dilly!" introduced in the Bud Light beer ads of 2017 and 2018. Random? Yes. Stupid? No more stupid than raising health with an Old French word meaning "countenance." But I don't believe that day, if it is coming, will take over our toast any time soon. "Cheers" has far too great a legacy, is far too popular, and is far too full of sentiment to be ousted anytime soon. To this classic, I'm happy to raise a glass any day.

TASTING NOTE
Jack Daniel's whiskey, West Coast wines (United States); London dry gin, Johnnie Walker scotch whiskey (United Kingdom); Penfolds wine (Australia).

"Terviseks"
(ter've'seks)
("To health")

Consider this: a group of
countries speaking more or
less the same language but calling them all by different names in
order to create separate national
identities. We see this in the Balkans, with Serbian and Croatian, and you'll find something similar with Ga-
lician as opposed
to Portuguese.

ESTONIAN

But now let's take the Baltics. Geographically, the northern Baltics fall on roughly the same longitude as the southern Balkans. Historically, you also find a similar struggle for identity.

How about linguistically? They're all Baltic countries, so they all speak a Baltic language. Kinda like in the Balkans? Not really. Technically there are two Baltic languages—Latvian and Lithuanian—and three Baltic states: those two plus Estonia. They all sit right on top of each other, and Latvian and Lithuanian grew up together, and together shared in the languages of old empires: Lithuanian, Polish, and Latvia Germanic. Which means they must be pretty close, right?

Here's a look at some Lithuanian: "Galiu kalbėti angliškai" ("I can speak English"). All right, so if Latvian is a cousin it ought to have something in common, but the Latvian is: "Varu runāt angļu valodā." So much for resemblance. Just for kicks, the same phrase in neighboring Estonian is "Ma oskan inglise keelt rääkida." "English" at least is recognizable in all three languages, but there's not a whole lot else.

Now if this generates nothing about Baltic languages except a headache, that at least goes to show that this part of the world is rather more language convoluted than elsewhere in Europe. Estonia, Latvia, and Lithuania are next to each other, and they're all classified in the same zone of countries. The language problem is that Estonian and Finnish emerged from beyond the Urals, Latvian from Proto-Indo-European tribes. And Lithuanian? Like Basque, it's been in the same place forever and is so conservative that some linguists have claimed it has more in common with Sanskrit than Polish, with whom it once ran a successful empire.

Drinking in Estonia, luckily, isn't near as complex as the language. Its capital Tallinn provides some of the most breathtakingly beautiful Gothic buildings in Europe. You can explore it at your leisure after sipping down a couple pints of Põhjala porter. The Põhjala brewhouse offers a variety of styles, flavored through a combination of long barrel aging and distinctive ingredients: the Leevike Spiced Winter Ale, for example, features fermented cranberries, hibiscus, honey, cinna-

mon, and cloves. If beer isn't your thing and you're looking to sample a good local spirit, give Vana Tallinn a whirl. This is a chocolate-colored rum-based liqueur flavored with citrus, caramel, toffee, warm spices, and vanilla.

Saying *terviseks* (to health) and keeping your eyes locked is the custom, and, yes, the *seks* is pronounced as you think it is. This occasions much amusement with tourists and has given rise to the popular (and naughtier) "Tervis sulle, seks mulle" (Health to you, sex to me).

10

FINNISH

"Kippis"
(kee'pays)
("Cheers")

While no one knows precisely from where or when *kippis* sprang up, Finns provide two theories. The first holds that the word was imported from the German expression *die Gläser kippen*, meaning "to tilt (the glasses) back." That fits rather nicely as following Finland's independence in 1917 and the subsequent civil war, there were a number of German migrants in Helsinki.

However, one may just as well prefer the second story, which comes from the Great Migration period between 1870 and 1930. Instead of wishing their neighbors "hello," Finnish immigrants preferred telling them to "keep peace."

Kippis a playful word and liberally used; however, if you crave something more challenging, try *pohjanmaan kautta* (down the hatch) or the more fun alternative *hölökyn kölökyn* (*hullykoon kullykoon*) three times fast. When you get this down, you're ready for the full exchange:

A: Hölökyn kölökyn.
B: Hölökynpä kölökyn. (Right! Down the hatch.)
A: Hölökynpä hyvinni kölökyn. (Truly, down the hatch indeed.)
If you don't think that's fun, you've got the wrong book.

Finland has a bevy of bizarre and interesting drinks, such as the sweet *lakka* (literally "cloudberry") liqueur and *sima*, a spring mead mixed with lemon, raisins, and dry yeast. Many people bemoan the high cost of alcohol in Finland (eight dollars a beer), but if you don't really care about where you drink, it's an easy problem to solve. Helsinki natives planning on a big carouse will cross the Gulf of Finland and smuggle in crates of beer from Estonia, where prices are comparatively cheaper.

So what's the story with Finnish? Like Hungarian and Estonian, its distant ancestor Proto-Finno Ungaric wandered in from the Urals somewhere in the ballpark of four thousand years ago. Also like its sisters, Finnish is famously sticky (in linguistics this is called agglutinative), meaning words pick up little pieces that designate parts of speech.

Example: "garden" is *puutarha*, "in the garden" is *puu-tarhassa*, and "in *my* garden" is *puutarhassani*.

The sticky Finnish language also has the fabulous trait of jerry-rigging words together to make completely new ones in a process called compounding. Many languages do this—German is famous for it—but Finnish compounding with its oceans of vowels and pattering, polysyllabic repetition both looks and sounds delightful. Take the word "telephone," *puhelin*, which provides the structure of a large phone-related syllabary, including words like "telemarketer," "phone booth," and "phone number." Put all this in a sentence, and what you wind up with is "Puhelinmyyjä on puhelinkotelossa ja hänen puhelinnumeronsa on" ("The telemarketer is in the phone booth, and his number is").

Compounding also has the habit of stringing together unrelated words for new concepts, like with the English "earphones" and "blackboard." But these are positively humdrum when set beside Finnish. Happy would the English compound become should it ever engender anything as wonderful as *hyppytyynytyydytys* ("bouncy cushion satisfaction.")

11

FRENCH

"Santé"
(sahn'tay)

("Health")

Le vin sait revêtir le plus sordide bouge
D'un luxe miraculeux,
Et fait surgir plus d'un portique fabuleux
Dans l'or de sa vapeur rouge,
Comme un soleil couchant dans un ciel
    nébuleux.

The wine knows how to put on the most
    sordid move
Of a miraculous luxury,
And brings up more than a fabulous portico
In the gold of his red vapor,
Like a setting sun in a cloudy sky.

—CHARLES BAUDELAIRE, "Le Poison"

45

Parmi les gazons
Tout en floraisons
Dessous les treilles,
J'écoute sans fin
La chanson du Vin
Dans les bouteilles.

Among the turf
While blooming
Under the trellises,
I listen without end
The Song of Wine
In the bottles

—THÉODORE DE BANVILLE, "La Chanson du Vin"

You don't go very long talking about French culture without mentioning wine. French verses honoring and cursing the vine are so numerous you could stock a good-sized library with them. Even just talking about wine forces you into an enormous French lexicon stuffed with words like *chateau*, *terroir*, *vintage*, and *sommelier*: originally, a term for a person in charge of leading the pack animals who schlepped provisions. And then, there are all those grapes: pinots, cabernets, chardonnay, champagne, sauvignon blanc, syrah, merlot, and, of course, Bordeaux, where French wines really get their start.

In the year 1154, the first Bordeaux craze struck when the English king Henry Plantagenet married into French royalty, plunging the country into a claret-fueled patriotic fever. This, Bordeaux's first big break, was followed by a second golden era right around the year 1701. The occasion was the War of Spanish Succession and the English boycott of that ever-so-popular fortified Spanish wine, sherry. During this time Bordeaux became so popular and the varieties so numerous, winemakers resorted to putting labels on their bottles to distinguish the region where the wine came from. This was and still is important because France was sending more and more of its wine overseas.

Bordeaux flourished throughout the eighteenth and nineteenth centuries and then came to sudden failure in the mid-1860s when the French wine blight struck. For almost a millennium the French had been steady wine drinkers, but with so much Bordeaux destroyed, tipplers needed to find a different alcohol to get their fix on. This marked the debut of French absinthe, a liquor that, to this day, is still infamous. For the next half century, France ran on an absinthe crave so vicious that Gustave Flaubert predicted it would end with the destruction of the French army. Absinthe didn't lead to the kinds of catastrophe prophesied by Flaubert, but bad absinthe (improperly brewed with poisonous additives) did its

TASTING NOTE
local wines and champagnes, pastis aniseed aperitif, absinthe.

fair share of damage. All the same, within the first twenty years of the twentieth century, following the rise of Prohibition in the United States, it had been banned on both sides of the Atlantic—the United States in the early 1900s and France in 1915. Prohibition ended in the United States in 1933, but absinthe was only legalized in 2007. As for France, the ban was officially lifted in 2011.

That would bring us to the modern age, and a pretty good age it is to be a French wine drinker and French speaker. Although French colonial power is a thing of the past, Francophone countries are to be found throughout Europe, the Caribbean, French Polynesia, in Quebecois Canada, and in twenty-six African countries. You can hear the same toast in any one of these countries—a clink of glasses with either the polite *à votre santé* (to your health) or simply *santé*. Equally popular in France is the short phrase *à la tienne* (to yours), and if you want to get a little more intricate, here's a nice drinking line: "Verre plein je te vide, verre vide je te plains" ("The full glass I'll empty, the empty I pity"). Whatever you go with, it all pairs equally well with a nice Bordeaux.

12

GALICIAN

"Saúde"
(soe'je)
("Health")

Take a look at the Iberian triptych. In the east we've got Catalan; in the middle, Castilian (modern) Spanish and Basque; and on the far western strip, we've got Portuguese.

Except that for much of the past thousand years, Portuguese was paired with a language called Galego, or Galician. In fact, it was only during the last century that Galician and Portuguese speakers finalized their divorce. What's the relationship like now? A bit like that of Dari and Farsi. The countries are right next to each other, speakers understand one another without much difficulty, and the languages are recognized as independent (they've got different names, don't they!) but are very similar, give or take some loan words and a different accent.

Galicia is also said to have hosted some Celtic Gallaeci back in the day, hence the modern Celtic influences in Galician music and even Gaelic sport. Granted, usually the Gaelicness of these sports should be taken with a grain of salt, but Galicia did field a 2012 Gaelic football team that defeated Breton-speaking Brittany.

If you end up visiting Galicia, it's more likely you'll remember the colorful festivals, fried *pulpo* (octopus), fragrant *albariño* wines, and the Cathedral of Santiago de Compostela. For at least a thousand years, pilgrims have made the arduous trek to Compostela, traversing many hundreds of miles on a pilgrimage that has become known as the Camino de Santiago—Way of Saint James. Paulo Coelho produced the most famous account of it in his novel *The Pilgrimage*, and Martin Sheen starred in the successful Camino-based *The Way* in 2010. The effects of media exposure have been enormous. In 2017 over 300,000 pilgrims walked it—compared with just 2,500 in 1986. As all good pilgrims know, anyone who marches six hundred miles through desert and then deluge is going to need a good celebration at the end.

Luckily, Galician red wines are many, and raised cups with cries of *saúde* are frequent. For something more meaningful and heartfelt, travelers may also raise a solemn toast *De hoxe nun ano*, roughly translated as "Same time next year?"

13

GERMAN

"Prost"
(proast)
("Cheers")

My mother keeps a pair of beer-swilling Bavarian muskrats on a shelf in her kitchen. The wife carries a pair of alpine skis. The husband wears a Tyrolean hat and hefts a sudsy stein. Press his foot, and he bobs up and down while singing this ditty: "Ein Prosit! Ein Prosit! Die Gemütlichkeit! Eins, zweo, drei, g'suffa!" which is something like "Cheers! Cheers! To comfort! One, two, three, chug!"

It's almost impossible to imagine any other country selling such a glorious piece of kitsch. Tourists would probably pay good money for a pair of swaggering French roosters with glasses of wine that chanted "Le Champs-Elysées," but this doesn't square with French dignity. I imagine the American equivalent as a couple of fat bulldogs in frat shirts barking "99 Bottles of Beer," but Americans are far too self-conscious about their drinking to promote such wanton merchandise. No, it is Germany and Germany alone where getting drunk can still be viewed as good clean fun.

There's most certainly no single answer for how this mentality has been able to persist, but I imagine Oktoberfest has had something to do with it. Also, a thousand years' worth of endorsements from the country's most luminous intellectuals and moral authorities have made beer drinking not just a happy pastime but a moral and intellectual prerogative. There's Johann Wolfgang von Goethe, who once kept his strength up during an illness by ingesting nothing but Köstritzer black beer, but writers and alcohol are too much of a cliché. "Who loves not women, wine, and song, remains a fool his whole life long": thus *sprach* Martin Luther, the most well-known religious reformer of all time and also Germany's most famous gastronome. Another aphorism of his goes like this: "A happy fart never comes from a miserable ass." (Farts seem to have been an eternal preoccupation with Martin Luther. In several of his many criticisms against the then pope Leo X, "pope fart-ass," he thunders with numerous "kiss-ass," "kiss-fart," "ass-lick," and worse insults.)

Religious orders have enjoyed a close relationship with brewing for at least fifteen hundred years—the beer-brewing monk is probably as much of a cliché as the alcoholic writer. More than a hobby, brewing for monks and nuns was a sign of progressiveness and ingenuity. The Benedictine abbess Hildegard von Bingen, of the twelfth century, in between her work as a composer, seer, conlanger, natural scientist, philosopher, and adviser to the German emperor Frederick Barbarossa, also

TASTING NOTE
kirschwasser fruit schnapps; Paulaner, Erdinger, and Hofbrau beers.

57

pioneered the use of hops in the brewing process. Suffice it to say beer has some pretty good advertisement.

Add to this that not only do Germans drink more than most everyone else (except for the Czechs and the Austrians); they drink in more places. Fun places. Everybody knows about the Hofbrauhaus of Munich, but many Americans have probably never gotten their fix on at a *Biergarten*. You can find these little slices of paradise all over the German-speaking countries (the big ones are Germany, Austria, and much of Switzerland) and in sundry locations across the world. Austria by the way has three different types: the traditional Biergarten, the more local *Buschenschank*, and the *Heuriger*, a Biergarten specializing in wine.

And toasts? Drinking involves plenty and none of them long-winded. Clink with a *prost*, and keep your eyes fixed on your companions'. Failure to look eye to eye is said to result in seven years' bad sex: a common curse around Europe. *Prost* derives from the Latin *prosit* (profit) and is perfect for most settings. If you want to be slightly more formal, consider the politer *Zum Wohl* (to your health).

One final word about alcohol. The red-cheeked man with the large mug is probably one of the most famous German mascots, but in reality, it is a Bavarian image, not German. Bavaria is a German state in the south whose people speak in a dialect much different from standard Hochdeutsch (High German). Some Germans may take offense at being associated with their tippling neighbors, and it would be wise to recognize the distinction.

14

GREEK

"Γεια μας"
(geia'mas)

("To your health")

TASTING NOTE
ouzo, raki, tsipouro,
and *tsikoudia*
pomace brandy;
Chios Mastiha
liqueur.

Ouzo: three thousand years of Greek culture masquerading as a shot. With the first drink, you and your buddies start out talking as big and wise as Socrates. By drink three, you're out of philosophy, and you may feel a little loftier and weightless, flying, if you will, like Aristophanes's birds of Cloud Cuckooland. This is the comic aspect of your Dionysia, and you will enjoy its fun, but sooner or later your evening starts to tailspin straight into tragedy. By ouzo number six, you'll be stumbling around like a blinded Cyclops, and by eight you'll be down for the count. The rest is history—which later your friends will partially fabricate and partially spice up to make for a more entertaining story, in the spirit of history's great father, Herodotus. Indeed, you might say that ouzo is as central to Greek culture as the Parthenon. OK, that's a stretch, but it's still pretty important, and as long as you keep your wits about, you won't end up boozed up, face to the floor.

Here's a short history (and compared to most other things Greek, it really is short). The first ouzo distillery opened its doors in 1856, twenty-four years after the Greek War of Independence was fought against the Ottoman Turks. The recipe came from a similar spirit called *tsipour*, sometimes flavored with anise, which had been brewed for centuries on Mount Athos. Timing was certainly on the side of the new spirit. After French absinthe was banned in 1915, ouzo was quick to swoop in and carry off the anise-loving tipplers. Thus, in about sixty years, ouzo went from new kid on the block to most popular spirit in the country. And not only that, but because of its proximity to Greek independence, it quickly became infused with the image of Greek nationality: to this day, it is the beverage of choice for celebrating Greek independence. Which is a little ironic because the word *ouzo* is taken either from the Turkic word for grape (*ūzūm*) or from an Italian customs stamp, *uso Massalia*, meaning "for use in Marseilles."

Ouzo drinking involves the simple but crucial step of adding water to the glass before drinking. As in related spirits like raki, absinthe, or Pernod, the water will react with the anise and produce a milky solution, which will make your drink that much more appetizing, as long as you don't overdo it.

Now it's ready to drink, but not with *opa*. *Γεια μας* (our health) is the standard toast, made with clinking glasses and broad smiles. If, perhaps, you find the whole "to health" business redundant, there's *eβιβα*" (*eh vee va*), a Latin loan meaning "to life" and also a few cleverer inspirations: *na psofisei o Haros* means "may Charon drop dead" (Charon being the boatman who ferried the dead to the underworld) and the self-reflective *na pane kato ta farmakia*, meaning "may the poisons go down."

15

HUNGARIAN

"Egészségedre"
(a'gey'shey'ga'dra)

("For your good health")

Warning: glass clinkers will be pro-
secuted. No joke. If you're bringing
out the *egészségedre* (for your good
health) and drinking beer, Hungari-
ans make a point to refrain from
bonking the vessels. The story
goes that when Hungary lost
its revolutionary war in 1848
to the Habsburg/Russian
alliance, thirteen of its
senior generals were
executed by Austrian
officers, who then
celebrated by conk-
ing their mugs together.

65

Those who witnessed the act were so angered by the gloating victors that they put a moratorium on the clink, which abides to this day. All in the name of patriotism.

The drinking formula dictates that following a first drink, you may then be asked to *igyunk pertut*," or "Drink a *pertu*," with your Hungarian acquaintances as a means of solidifying your relationship. Pertu is not some sort of local throat-tightening firecracker, and to *pertut inni* does not necessitate drinking alcohol or even drinking anything called *pertu*. *Pertu*, according to many, isn't even Hungarian but a word derived from the Latin *per tu* (by you), and in fact, there might not be any drinking involved in your pertu whatsoever. Drinking pertus indicates that you and your companions have officially passed over the stranger/friends threshold and can start being familiar with each other, a process abiding under the elegant name of *te-ként, te megszólítás szerint*, which in Hungarian means that you start calling each other by your first names and change out pronouns from the formal to the friendly. If we still said "thou" in English, now would be the time to whip it out.

Successfully finish your pertu, and you're ready to move on to cheers. Congratulations! It's time for *legkedvesebb megegesegesedesunkre* (our most beloved affliction)! What is this affliction? One final ritual, generally postpertu, during which you cross arms with your companion and take a shot of Hungarian aqua vitae, *pálinka*. Drinking pálinka really *does* entail drinking, and some discretion is advised. Pálinka is a traditional fruit brandy a lot like schnapps. Put down a few shots, and you may feel a little more Hungarian and definitely a whole lot dizzier.

TASTING NOTE
pálinka fruit brandy, Dreher beer, Tokaj and local wines.

"Sláinte"
(slahn'che)
("Health")

Craic: Irish term for gossip, entertainment, good social activity, or anything fun

Ex: "What's the craic?"
"Oh, the craic is grand."
How's it going?
It's alright.

Using any search engine you prefer, type in "blessing pillow" or something like it, and scroll through the images until you come across an Irish blessing. Found it? Good—it should take about three seconds. Now scroll through your options until you come across a German blessing. Takes a while, doesn't it? But why? Germany's population is at least twenty times that of Ireland, and Germans make up an enormous percentage of immigrants in the United States. Is German English simply not as sonorous as the Irish? Martin Luther would disagree. Thing is, no one can reason why Irish culture, particularly its *word culture*, has such seduction, staying power, and enchantment. The blessings are just as good in Irish as they are in English, and they have the added benefit of doubling down as toasts. They're as good a place to start as anywhere.

Here's one to whet your whistle: "Go mbeirimíd beo ar an am seo arís" (*Guh me-imeed byoh er an am shoh areesh*; May we be alive this time next year). Or how about this toast, containing those three quintessential Irish themes, Ireland, booze, and death: "Fad saol agat, gob fliuch, agus bás in Éirinn" (*Fad sayal awgut, gub fluk agus bawss in Ayrinn*; May you have a long life, a wet mouth, and may you die in Ireland).

Now just wait a minute. What's all this Irish business about? Doesn't everyone in Ireland speak English? This business is a long story, which

I will let your man in the pub tell you over a pint or two of Guinness. Suffice it to say that there is an Irish language, sometimes called Irish Gaelic, sometimes just Irish, with a relative in Scotland and some distant cousins on the European mainland. Irish owes its amazing quasi-Dracula resurrection from the dead to some resilient speakers among the country's rural population, compulsory education, and the valiant efforts of some organizations to give this aged (over 2,500 years!) language a face lift. Just to name one: students from the Irish-speaking high school Coláiste Lurgan have a music project called TG Lurgan, which records Irish-language interpretations of popular songs from artist such as Ed Sheeran, Luis Fonsi, and Lady Gaga. Their YouTube videos have garnered millions of views. More importantly, they've also demonstrated how to use pop culture to resurrect a dead language in a modern day and age.

So that's the Irish language in a nutshell, but what's Irish in a glass? *Sláinte*, quick and easy, or *Sláinte agus saol agat* (*slahnche ohgus seel ag'at*), "health and long life to you," for a little more complicated. Libations? Guinness and Jameson whiskey, as if you didn't know already. As English dominates the urban plain, your best option to hear some Irish is in the west and northwest countryside, and in these small rural communities, "sessions," or informal music recitals, are a staple of local culture. Get yourself into a good pub, and soak it all up.

TASTING NOTE
Guinness,
Bulmers cider,
poitín/craythur
(moonshine).

17

ITALIAN

"Saluti," "Cin-Cin"
(salute), (chin-chin)

("Health," "Cheers")

Italy is home to some of the most widely enjoyed cocktails and wines in the world. Additionally, it boasts arguably some of the best aperitifs known to man, from prosecco to Campari to Aperol. Wines are immensely popular, as well, including those made from muscat of Alexandria, considered one of the oldest grapes still being cultivated.

TASTING NOTE
Moreno, Moretti,
and Peroni beers;
grappa; prosecco
and local wines
(primitivo and
Valpolicella).

Italy contains a staggering amount of rich and diverse wines, and visitors can find just about anything pleasing to their palette. Try a sample of *primitivo* wines, progeniture of the tannic zinfandel popular on both sides of the Atlantic. Or, if you've got a bit more to spend, shell out for a bottle with the Valpolicella appellation: grapes here are semi-dried to produce the region's most famous production, the singular and intense "raisin wine" known as Amarone.

Italian toasting is easy enough. Lift your glass, lock eyes, and say one of three things: *saluti*, prost, or *cin-cin*. The first two terms date back to the Roman Empire, and many European toasts (excluding the Slavics) share the same roots from the Latin *salutem* (health) or *prosit* (to be of use).

Romans were notorious boozers during their day, but then so was everyone else. What makes them interesting is that they effected a complete 180-degree turn in just thirty years, going from being a sober culture that slaughtered its drunks to one whose emperors would be writing the first wine-making textbooks. Romans evidently loved talking about wine as much as they loved drinking it. The historian Cato the Elder and natural philosophers Varro and Pliny (also Elder) spend pages upon pages extolling it.

When the ADs began, the Roman Empire received the works of Columella, who provided not only the most extensive wine list then known but who can also be credited with popularizing a wine vocabulary. Which just goes to show that in addition to concrete, the aqueduct, and the modern calendar, the Roman Empire also invented the first wine talk. Feeling chilly? Have a sip of a "wooly Aminean." Or perhaps you'd care for something stronger? In that case, this "full-breasted Bumast" will suit you fine.

A plethora of drinks calls for a plethora of toasts, and third on the list is the popular cin-cin (sometimes *chin-chin*). Probably an onomatopoeia for the clinking of the glasses, it might also be a loanword from Japanese (ちんちん), brought over by merchant sailors. It means "penis." How or why this word was chosen as the basis for a ritual professing fellowship

and camaraderie escapes the knowledge of many, though travelers need not blush when raising their glass. Japanese tourists, on the other hand, may feel a little strange, though in the words of one traveler: If they want to raise a toast to my penis, who am I to say no? When in Rome.

18

LATVIAN

"Priekā," "Uz veselibu"
(preeka), (ooz vesel'iboo)
("Cheers," "To health")

Latvian and Lithuanian are a bit like that couple you see waddling down the street, the ones who've been married for a century and who've grown so close they speak language between them absolutely nobody else can understand. In fact, you're not even sure *they* can understand one another.

Here's a Latvian talking about his bundle of twigs: "Šis žagaru saišķis nav mans žagaru saišķis" ("This bundle of sticks is my bundle of sticks"). And here comes a Lithuanian with a mention of her six geese: "Šešios žąsys su šešiais žąsyčiais" ("Six geese with six goslings"). Fun, right? Trying to speak a Baltic language is like doing backflips with your tongue. It also didn't help that in the end of the thirteenth century, Latvia was overrun by the German-speaking Brothers of the Sword, who effectively severed any contact between the two Baltic languages, which might have resulted in greater mutual intelligibility.

Well, what about Estonian? It's just a bit north, so it'd be logical to think it shares some commonalities with its neighbor. Logical yes, but not at all the case. Spend thirty seconds listening to speakers of Latvian and Estonian and the language gap becomes clear as a glass of vodka. Vodka, incidentally, while not a Latvian invention, is a huge export. Stolichnaya has its headquarters in Riga, which is a good place to get your toast on. The Latvian *veselibas* (health) provides the underlying structure, and the whole phrase *uz veselibu* means "to your health," said with the typical clank of mugs or glasses. More efficient is the word *priekā*, which is closer to the simple "cheers."

Alcoholic drinks in Latvia typically resemble those of other Eastern European countries, and although there is a good selection of regional beers to sample (Cesu, Aldaris, or Bauskas), tourists might consider a shot of Riga Black Balsam, a little firecracker Latvians have been brewing for 260 years. This bittersweet herbal mixture infused in pure vodka can

be served mixed with schnapps (unlikely but possible), soda, and even ice cream, depending on your preference.

If you have any trouble wrapping your tongue around Latvian toasts after a few too many Black Balsams, you can trade the words out for the simpler *sveiks* (*svayks*), meaning both "cheer" and "hello."

19

LITHUANIAN

"Į sveikatą"
(ee svay'kata)

("Bless you")

Trivia time! Which of the following is the name of a famous British playwright? Frydrichas Nyčė or Viljamas Šekspyras? Pretty kooky, right? It gets better. If *futbolas* is "football" and *kokteilis* is "cocktail," then "hamburger" is . . .? *Mėsainis*! Printer? *Spausdintuvas*. Media? *Žiniasklaida*.

Turns out Lithuanizing words isn't quite an exact science. Even so, incorporating twenty-first-century vocabulary into a six-thousand-year-old language is a bit like your great-grandmother getting a job with Geek Squad. Impossible? Certainly not, but once she's there, everything's going to be done her way or not be done at all.

Lithuanian is famous for being the oldest surviving Proto-Indo-European (PIE) language in the world, or the language with the most PIE-like traits. For nonlinguists, technology around the time of the late PIE era (Early Middle Bronze Age: 3,000–2,500 BC) amounted to camels, bronze, and mummies. Typically, when we think of ancient languages, we think of Sanskrit or Mycenean Greek, but Lithuanian has got more PIE than any of them. A word-by-word rundown would be tedious, so here are just a few examples. PIE "chin" is *smek*, compared with Lithuanian *smakras*. "Snow" is *sneig*, compared with Lithuanian *snigti*. And PIE "to eat" is *edmi*, compared with Lithuanian *edu*. PIE "cheers"? If only!

Į sveikatą is the word in Lithuania. And as for drinks when exploring the stunningly gorgeous Vilnius (sometimes called the "Jerusalem of the North"), you're going to want to take plenty of pit stops to sit down, admire the architecture, and sip something refreshing. Volfas Engelman, Dundulis, and Vilkmerges have popular beers that are drunk widely.

If you're in the mood for something special, try getting your hands on a glass of *krupnikas* (in Polish *krupnik*, which is both a savory soup

and spirit), first brewed in 1593. This honey liquor is generally served around the holidays or at traditional festivals and packs a fragrant punch, like potpourri in a glass. Flavors include honey (a given) along with cinnamon, nutmeg, cloves, vanilla, orange, and lemon peel. Some producers also flavor the spice-laden beverage with ginger, caraway, cardamom, and even saffron.

For a truly traditional Lithuanian drinking experience, however, sample some good old-fashioned mead—*midus*, in Lithuania, for the golden color of its honey. Mead was the ancient world's drink of choice, and although its popularity has fallen off in most countries, the mead train in Lithuania has actually been picking up speed.

20

MALTESE

"Saħħa"
(sah'ha)
("Health")

As linguistic red herrings go, there
are the glaring (Basque), the subtle
(Lithuanian), and the subtle subtle,
to which Maltese proudly belongs.
An American audience can be forgiven for not knowing much
about the language of
this sub-Italian
paradise.

TASTING NOTE
Stretta IPA,
Cisk Lager,
and other
local beers;
regional wines.

Sure, there was *The Maltese Falcon*, but Bogart speaks about as much Maltese in that as he speaks Arabic in *Casablanca* or, for that matter, as much Kazakh as Sacha Baron Cohen speaks in *Borat*.

A European audience may be forgiven for thinking Maltese a romance language, but at 70 percent Italian and French, it's pretty darn close to being one. Grammar and family tree make this language a close relative of Arabic, which isn't difficult to believe when you hear the Maltese, roughly 90 percent Catholic, refer to God as Allah.

Maltese is a bit like the iPhone of languages, forced to reformat and repackage every few years. This was historically whenever a new conqueror blew through. For better or worse, the empires that invaded it were all the cream of their respected crops: Phoenicians, Romans, Arabs, and Norman Sicilians just for starters.

Things got more complex for the Maltese language when the Holy Roman Emperor Charles V gave the island to the homeless Hospitaliiers (Knights of Malta) in 1530. With both feet through the Maltese door, the order summarily dumped a sizeable portion of Italian into what was then a dialect of Arabic. A few centuries later, Napoleon dropped by for a visit and left some French behind when the British chased him away.

That was two hundred years ago, and the British haven't left since: along with Italy and France, they account for most of the country's tourism. While, as of now, there isn't a Maltese "prost," travelers are just as likely to hear "cheers" as *saħħa* or *evviva* (cheers).

As a southern European country with a hot, arid climate, viticulture flourishes in Malta, with Delicata wines leading the way: they produce sweet and crisp whites as well as full-bodied and sparkling reds. For beer, Cisk Lager is one of the most popular brews.

21

NORWEGIAN

"Skål"
(skol)
("Toast")

Norwegian loanwords are easily spotted in English. *Fjord* and *floe* take little linguistic training to recognize. There's a kind of curveball with the word *ski*, but *slalom* (not-too-fast downhill skiing) and *klister* (ski wax) are decidedly foreign, as is the *skrei* (crowd) of fish terms: *brisling*, *krill*, and *lutefish*. If you fall off your *yngling* (small boat) or wipe out trying to execute a complex telemark (ski turn) you might say, "Uff da!"

And Norwegian even has its own term for a Benedict Arnold—a *quisling*. This sounds a little humdrum, but it ought to be mentioned that Norwegian also gave English its *kraken* and its *narwhal*, two sea-dwelling, alienesque creatures of mythological proportions. The kraken was a giant squid that dragged merchant ships to the bottom of the sea, according to Jules Verne, Herman Melville, and Captain Jack Sparrow. The narwhal is an arctic-dwelling whale masquerading as a unicorn. They're the ones responsible for all the unicorn horns you find in old museums. There's even a whole throne made of "unicorn horn" in Copenhagen. But back to the list.

You might guess from it that Norwegians are a laid-back people with a fondness for skiing, sailboats, and salty fish, and you'd be exactly right. According to the World Economic Forum, it's a close match between the Finns and the Norwegians in terms of who are the happiest people in the world.

While there are all kinds of hypotheses about what makes the world's happiest people so happy (I imagine it has something to do with also being named one of Europe's most beautiful countries by *Travel Away*), there's an idea that Norway's restrictive alcohol laws might play a part. This starts with prices. A standard Norwegian beer generally costs between six and ten bucks. Young Norwegians usually avoid getting drunk at bars, and if they go to a supermarket, they have to buy their beer before 8:00 p.m. Wine Monopoly (Vinmonopolet)—the only outlet where you can buy stuff over 4.75 percent—closes even earlier, at 6:00 p.m. That sounds awfully restrictive. Hell, it *is* restrictive, but Norwegians seem to like it this way: 80 percent of people voted to keep their Vinmonopolet, rather than change to a more liberal system, according to a 2016 survey.

Does less opportunity equal less drinking? Logically yes, but drinking is still done with gusto, albeit more often at house parties and home settings. All the usual spirits are brought out for casual consumption, but for special toasts and holidays you may be introduced to *akevitt* (from *aqua vitae*), a grain spirit flavored with anise, cumin, cardamom, caraway, fennel, or orange, and sipped, not chugged.

For a quiet toast, there's the simple *skål*, but before you take shots, don't be freaked out if Norwegians break out into song. Actually, feel free to join in: the most popular is "Ol, øl og mere øl," and the only thing you need to know before belting it out is that *øl* is "beer" and *og mere*, "one more." Happy countries, simple pleasures.

TASTING NOTE
pils and export beers, akevitt, schnapps.

22

POLISH

"Na zdrowie"
(na zdro'vihye)

("To health")

Mix together the most common Polish loanwords, and you can have yourself a pretty good meal. There's kielbasa for your protein, pierogi for your carbs, and gherkins (cucumber) for your veggies.

For washing that meal down, you might like some to krupnik, which is technically vodka but so flushed with honey and herbs that your friends, if you're a man, might make fun of you for drinking it. Żubrówka Bison Grass vodka ranks high in popularity, followed shortly after by Żołądkowa Gorzka, literally "bitter vodka for the stomach." There's also Goldwasser (once known as Gdanska Wodka, or "Vodka of Gdansk"). Distilled from potatoes and mixed with anise, mint, and pepper, this sweet and spicy liqueur has been around since the end of the sixteenth century and really does contain pieces of gold leaf: a sixteenth-century recipe used by medieval alchemists as a clever marketing strategy to entice rich boozers and frivolous sorority girls. In 2009, however, Goldwasser moved production from Poland to Germany, so technically we oughtn't to include it in our list of Polish things.

Polish includes many sweet, good things, however, like many Slavic languages, this downtrodden Slavic tongue has a rather unsavory reputation when it comes to pronunciation. To be fair, there seems to be no Slavic language with a particularly positive reputation (compare adjectives used to describe French, Italian, and Spanish to those used for Slovak or Russian. Or compare the tinkling sound of French *santé* to the consonant forest in the Russian "hello," *zdravstvuyte*). But it comes down like a hammer on poor Polish. This is almost entirely due to Polish spelling. Take the word "ruthless" (*bezwzględny*), stick it on the Polish name Grzegorz Brzęczyszczykiewicz (a hero in a World War II drama), say he's in the village of Szymankowszczyzna, and you get "Bezwzględny Grzegorz Brzęczyszczykiewicz w Szymankowszczyzna." You like that? Here, have another! "W Szczebrzeszynie chrząszcz brzmi w trzcinie" (In Szczebrzeszyn a beetle sounds in the reeds). Toasting is much simpler: you say *na zdrowie*, "to (your) health," and raise a respectful glass.

The vodka flows plentifully throughout Eastern Europe, but if the prospect of slugging down a few hard shots doesn't appeal to you, there are some other options, like Podpiwek, Polish kvass (rye beer). Suitable for the lightweights, the name literally means "subbeer." For shots, you go with *nalewka*—an aged slightly-sweeter-than-schnapps liquor available in many different flavors.

TASTING NOTE
Podpiwek
kvass, nalewka
schnapps,
Żubrówka Bison
Grass vodka.

"Saúde"
(so'jee)

("Bless you")

Ever wonder how things got to have
the names they did? The Americas,
for example, come from the name
of the Italian merchant Amerigo
Vespucci, whose sole contribution to history lies in the
fact that he recognized
the Americas were not
Asia. He didn't need
to do much: just call
them by a different
name. What goes
in a name?
In the case of the Americas,
some geographical irony.

23

PORTUGUESE

TASTING NOTE
ginja cherry liquor,
Dois Corvos beers,
Madeira, and
fortified port
wines.

But Portugal has got quite a bit more history. The name itself is a bastardization of the Latinized name for an ancient city sitting on the mouth of the Douro River, Portus Cale. Two thousand years ago it was inhabited by the Callaeci, or Gallaeci, the Celtic people inhabiting Gallicia and Portugal until Caesar Augustus decided he'd put a stop to that. Including *Portus* in the name of the country was a nifty way of indicating that this country sat on water, but it was also a prophetic reference to Portugal's future maritime empire, which kicked off with the acquisition of Brazil in 1500 and fizzled out in 1999, with the return of Macau to China.

But the Portuguese language endures abroad, more successfully than any colonial language except English and Spanish. That's certainly obvious when it comes to Brazil where Portuguese speakers outnumber those in Portugal sixteen to one (I've also heard eighteen to one), but Portuguese is still an official language in ten countries and survives as either a dialect or pidgin in places like Macau and Sri Lanka (and in Malaysia, where it's known as Kristang due to the many Portuguese-speaking Christian missionaries there).

Colonial exuberance equals lots of time on sea plus bad conditions, which equals lots of time and variables for exported weak wine to go bad. Portuguese brewers, like the Spanish, solved this problem by increasing the alcohol content in their wines, which led to the fortified wine known as *porto*, still enjoyed with dessert to this day. (The Spanish version was called *sack*, from the Spanish verb *sacar*, "to export," but in England it's now known as "sherry.") There are plenty of good port wines to sample in Portugal, and a thimble of Douro Valley Porto might be just what you want.

Portuguese speakers use both *saúde* (cheers) and *tin-tin* for their toasts, and they also lock eyes with their partners. A drunken outing with nothing but port sounds like an awful idea, however. Dois Corvos beers are popular and will provide a nice counterbalance to a heavy wine. There's

also the ever so popular *ginjinha*, a liquor distilled from sour cherries (*ginja*) and served with a piece of fruit. The best place to try your cup of ginjinha in Portugal is in the picturesque town of Óbidos, where the liquor is served in a cup made entirely out of chocolate.

ROMANIAN

"Noroc"
(no'roak)
("Good luck")

Romanian is a lonely language. As might be guessed from the name, its nearest relative is Italian, but Italy is a good eight hundred miles away, and what lies between is an island of misfit languages: Ukrainian in the north, Hungarian in the west, Serbian and Bulgarian in the south, and Moldova in the east, where Romanian is spoken but just as often as Russian or the Turkish off-shoot Gagauz.

To complicate matters, Romanian is constantly being confused with Roma, or Romani, the language of the Romani people of Indian Punjab with whom it shares absolutely nothing in common.

Bram Stoker gave Romania some welcome publicity when he resurrected one of the country's less savory historical personages and stuck him in the novel *Dracula*, a name that can be neatly divided to satisfy two cultures. *Dracul* is Romanian for "devil," but Stoker, an Irish writer, might have intended the Irish *drochfhuil* (the *fh* is silent), meaning "bad blood."

Either way you lean, it wouldn't be a bad idea to pick up a handy exorcism when wandering around the country of the Dracul. These come ready-packaged as toasts, one of which is *Doamne Ajută* (*dwomnay ajoota*), meaning "may God help us." More common is *sănătate* (*sana'tate*, "health"). *Noroc*, translated as "good luck," is probably bandied about the most. It can be said with a simple raise of the glass—no eye contact or clink required.

Chances are that you might hang around the Carpathian Mountains during your travels or even make it over to Transylvania for some castles and country charm. Village people are much more hospitable than sanguinary counts, and if you make the right friends, you might be treated to a traditional Romanian meal of *mititei* (dish of grilled ground meat rolls), *sarmale* (cabbage rolls), *mămăligă* (yellow maize porridge), or *ciorbă* (sour meatball soup). Celebratory shots will be of *țuică* (*tsuj'ke*), a liqueur distilled from plums and other fruits. Slam down a few of these babies, and you'll be out for the count. Better to take things slowly and maybe start off with a glass of two of Avincis sauvignon blanc, the toast of modern Romanian viticulture.

TASTING NOTE
țuică liqueur,
regional wines.

25

RUSSIAN

"За здоровье" *(za zdarov'ye)*

("To health")

In the Soviet comedy *Kidnapping, Caucasian Style*, the protagonist, Shurik, takes a holiday in the Caucasus to study myths, legends, and toasts. However, the locals only give him their toasts with the caveat that he drinks to each of them, a deal he regrets within the film's first ten minutes.

It's a terrific movie for a number of reasons, one of which is that it includes the catchiest song about bears since "Teddy Bear's Picnic," and also because those first ten minutes are the perfect guide toward giving a good Russian toast.

Za zdravo'ye (not to be confused with the Polish *na zdrowie* or Czech *na zdraví*) is your go-to word for quick clinks. While it's a passable toast for tourists, it won't be turning any of those famous Russian frowns upside down. *Za droozhboo* (friendship), *za vas* (to you), and *za lyoo'bov* (to love) are acceptable but far from ideal. The biggest country on earth is the home of the Faberge Egg, the Hermitage Museum, Tchaikovsky, and the thousand-page novel. Suffice it to say that Russians have a soft spot for displays of grandeur. Short of reciting Pushkin, one of the best ways to make a good impression is to stand, extend your glass, declare that you have a toast (*oo myen'ya yest toast*), make eye contact, and then state what is to be honored. If you really want to be a showoff, you can memorize one of the toasts from *Kidnapping*. Your Russian friends will certainly have seen it, and the toasts cover all kinds of ground, from the proverbial ("may our wishes always match our means") to the political ("may we never break ties with the work collective") to the enigmatic ("to cybernetics").

Toasting can be done with any drink you prefer—Georgian wine and beer such as Baltika 7 or Nevsky are both popular—but most tourists will probably want to sample the vodkas. This doesn't necessarily entail frat party pulls (but it can). Hotels and restaurants often offer samplings from a variety of vodkas, from top shelf Beluga and Russian Standard to cheaper brands. The portions are usually double shots and come with complimentary snacks (*za'koozkee*), such as cucumber, pickled herring, and assorted salads.

26

SERBIAN

"Живели," "Živeli"
(zhi've'lee)

("Cheers")

Looking at some of our modern-day modern vampires, you may be reminded of the collection of studs you see in early stages of *The Bachelorette*. You've got your bad boys (Gary Oldman, Christopher Lee), your pretty boys (Tom Cruise, Alexander Skarsgård), and usually the curveball: the engineer or computer programmer. These would be the Nosferatus and Count Orlock and, my personal favorite, Count von Count.

109

TASTING NOTE
rakia, Pelinkovac
wormwood liqueur,
Jelen and Lav beers,
regional wines.

What has any of this to do with Serbian? Well, there's the fact that the word *vampire* is imported from Serbian *vampir*. And then there's the fact that for any true vampire fans, your best bet of coming across the fabled bloodsucker is in the woods and mountains of Serbia.

If you were in Serbia in 2012, you might have run across an article entitled, "Vampire Threat Terrorizes Village." What happened was that an old water mill in the western Serbian village Zarozje collapsed. That's not news in and of itself, but the mill was alleged to be the home of the local demon Sava Savanović. With Savanović homeless and presumably on the hunt for a new nesting ground, villagers weren't taking any chances, and they promptly stocked up on crosses, icons, garlic, and hawthorn stakes to ward off the terror. The danger was reported to have lasted seven months. No vampire-related deaths came of the incident . . . that we know of.

This ought not to sound far-fetched if you compare vampire-related incidents in the former Yugoslavia with bigfoot sightings in the current United States. And like Sasquatch, Serbian vampires are deliciously marketable for tourists. If you're vampirephilo or just in the neighborhood, consider inquiring if any local terrorizers are buried nearby before you hammer away at the local brew.

This would be *rakija*, but in Serbia there's no such thing as just plain rakijia. When it's from plums, it's *sljivovica*; pear rakija is *viljamovka*;

grape, *loza*; and quince, *dunjovaca*. *Travarica* is rakija with herbs and loza; bitter rakija is *pelinkovac*, and honey rakija is *medovaca*. You got all that?

For those who have plans on trekking over to neighboring Bosnia, Croatia, or Montenegro and are looking to economize on your vocabulary, you're in luck. *Živeli* is "cheers" in all four countries (although Serbia will sometimes use the Latin alphabet, because—reasons). Macedonia is the exception to the one-word-fits-all rule, but hey, variety is the spice of language! Be sure to keep eye contact when raising your glass.

27

SLOVAK

"Na zdravie"
(na zdrav'ee)

("To health")

What's it like being a Slavic language?
Foreigners think you're too difficult to
learn, what with that funky alphabet
(Bulgarian, Ukrainian, Russian,
Serbian), mountainous words
with prickly consonants
(Polish), and a heavy,
archaic grammar
(all of them).

TASTING NOTE
Tatratea tea
liqueur,
borovička
juniper liqueur,
slivovica
plum liqueur.

Your reputation is that you're either always angry or playing the villain in an American action movie. Finally, you're enough like your brothers and sisters that no one takes you seriously as your own language unless you've got fifty million speakers or more.

So how does a language promote itself in peacetime? If you're Slovakia, you hire a man like Ľudovít Štúr, a Slovak nationalist and grassroots organizer so famous his profile appeared on the Slovak 500 koruna note in the 1990s and early 2000s. In roughly a decade of work cut short by a hunting accident, Štúr succeeded in codifying the fledgling tongue, choosing a central dialect (Slovak), drawing up a comprehensive grammar, and making the conscious decision to abolish the use of Czech in literary writing. (If that doesn't sound like much, try writing an official paper without using any Latin-based words.)

Why is this important? Well, if you're a marginalized Slavic language who's spent nearly a millennium under the thumb of a bully empire (Hungarian, Habsburgs), emerged on the tail of an uncomfortable hyphen, and was then suddenly thrust into autonomy in 1993, you'd probably say it's about time for people to start calling you by your proper name. Slovakia may not yet compare to its brother Czech Republic in popularity now, but this is changing. Like Prague and Budapest, Bratislava is becoming a prime spot for younger travelers due to its rich history, medieval architecture, and relatively low costs. Likewise, the Tatras mountain range is just now beginning to reach out to hikers who want to see white-capped mountains without paying Swiss prices.

As for toasts, looking eye to eye and clinking glasses with every drink is routine. As the best toasts come in threes, here's a nice one to get you started: "Na zdravie, na štastie, na lásku" ("To health, to luck, to love"). It's a handsome toast and may earn you a free shot of plum brandy, or *slivovica*. Rakia in all its forms (pear, plum, quince, herb, etc.) is drunk here as the national beverage, though if you're not the biggest fan of liqueurs, Zlatý Bažant beer is a popular choice for a good night out. There is also a popular Slovak version of gin, called *borovička*, from the Slovak word for juniper (*borievka*).

28

SLOVENIAN

"Na zdravje"
(na zdrav'ye)

("To health")

On the night of October 19, 1904, after a hectic two days of borrowing money and shuffling between Paris and London, the writer James Joyce and Nora Barnacle, the woman he's eloped with, arrive in Ljubljana. Under the impression that they are in Trieste, Joyce and Nora start off into the city, realizing their mistake only after the last train has left the platform.

The bedraggled couple is forced to spend the night in the park, which, uncomfortable as it no doubt was, earns them a commemorative plaque at the Ljubljana train station roughly a century later. Misadventures have turned out worse.

To Joyce's credit, Ljubljana was then known as Laibach, but the question remains, how do you confuse a name like Laibach with Trieste? How do you confuse a language like Slovenian with Italian, especially when you've got the language abilities of James Joyce? It turns out it's easier than it sounds. Slovenian Istria in the far west (just south of where Joyce thought he was) is so inundated with Italians that Italian is one of the region's official languages. Slovenia and languages have a very inclusive relationship. Like Romania, it's a stranger in a strange land, surrounded by Austrian German, Hungarian, Croatian, and Italian. Pace Croatian, they all come from completely separate families.

And then there's Slovene's rather glaring dialect issue. Language homogeny is something most Americans take for granted: in France there's French, Spain Spanish, England English, and so on—nothing more to it. When we come across a dialect, we assume it's no more than a quaint rephrasing, like "trolley" for "cart" and "holiday" for "vacation." But dialects mean much more: in China, for instance, its more than two hundred dialects can comprise completely different languages, as separate as English from Dutch. China's billion and a half people speaking two hundred dialects equals a different dialect per seven million people.

And Slovenia? With a population of just two million, Slovenian speakers carry on in approximately fifty different dialects, one per forty thousand. Amid huge landmasses such as China, linguistic diversity is something of a given. Slovenian may be deficient in area, but mountains—the Karawanks, the Julians, and the Kamnik-Savinja Alps—provide some of the best natural language barriers you can find.

If you're planning on taking an expedition to Slovenia, just remember it's bad form to drink before you've toasted (most often *na zdravje*) everyone at your table. And the looking eye-to-eye rule is enforced by the threat of seven years' bad sex.

As for drinks, this line from the Slovenian poet France Prešeren puts it pretty darn well: "Here sweet wine makes, once again, sad eyes and hearts recover." These sweet reds vary on location. *Rumeni muškat* (*moscato*), *malvazija*, and *rebula* are produced in the Primorska region of the far west. Along the coast there is *teran*, a dark red thought to have special medicinal properties. Finally, in the Lower Carniola (southeast) there is the blend Cvicek, a light, dry red with a relatively low alcohol content.

TASTING NOTE
Zganje local schnapps; Zelen, Pinela and Pikolit regional wines; HumanFish Reservoir Dogs craft beers.

29

SPANISH

"Salud"
(sa'lude)

("Health")

Big languages are often the results of big compromises. Look
no further than English and its
still-rocky relationship to the
Norman French that invaded
England almost a millennium
ago (rocky because anyone
liable to prefer "pensive"
to "thoughtful," "confec-
tionary" to "candy," or
"inquire" to "ask" is
either shady,
snobby, or
more likely
both).

Snobbery is also associated with the huge seepage of Latin words into English around the fifteenth and seventeenth centuries, providing gems like "juvenile," "pernicious," and "dexterity."

The pie of European Spanish is likewise a three-part split. There's Galician from the west, Catalan from the east, and Castilian (sometimes called Old Spanish) from the center. Although the languages balk at one other and Catalan speakers resent switching to Spanish from their native tongue, any language capable of converting a territory as massive as South America has to be pretty well organized. When Spanish conquistadors began arriving in the New World during the middle of the sixteenth century, they faced a language challenge that would make even the most devoted missionary blanch.

In 1892, after three and a half centuries of research, scholars concluded that in the Americas the total number of languages was about 490. These numbers turned out to be woefully low. In Mexico alone, there were 350 languages, and throughout the rest of the continent the number was around 2,000. It is thanks to the diligence and scholarship of Spain's missionaries, rather than its bloodthirsty conquistadors, that Spanish was able to take root in the continent.

Latin American Spanish and Castilian Spanish have their differences in pronunciation and loanwords, but *salud* (health) is used on both sides of the Atlantic. If you're in a rush, you couple the word with a clink, and that's all there is, but your drinking companions will probably want something more. So here's what you do: Raise your glass to the level of your forehead and say: "Arriba." Lower it and say: "Abajo." Move it out with *al centro*, and drink it down with *pa dentro*. That's a good wholesome toast, but there are plenty of naughtier ways to down a drink.

Many European languages threaten seven years' bad sex for failing to look eye to eye, and Spanish also has gleeful ways of imposing itself on your love life. Set your glass on the table and declare, "Quien no apoya, no folla," which is something like "He who doesn't put it down doesn't get laid." For a more formal affair, a longer toast (or to *hacer un brindis*) to long life, friendship, and love would be more appropriate than *salud* or the *arriba* routine. Sentimental or raunchy—any will do, although the better toasts would try to include both: "La mujer de otro hombre, en cuyos brazos pase los mejores momentos de mi vida . . . mi madre!" ("A toast to another man's woman in whose arms I've spent the best moments of my life . . . my mother!")

Lastly, I mentioned that some Catalan speakers prefer their own tongue over Spanish. "Cheers" is the same word, but to really honor your (male) companions, raise a glass with the words "Salut, i força al canut," or "Strength to the big cigar." I'll let you translate "big cigar."

30

SWEDISH

"Skål"
(skol)
("Bowl")

Sjung hopp faderallan allan lej,
Helan går, [*drink*] sjung hopp faderallan lej,
Och den som inte helan tar
Han heller inte halvan får,
Helan går, sjung hopp faderallan lej!

Sing hup fol-de-rol la la la la,
It all goes down, [*drink*] sing hup
   fol-de-rol la la,
And he who doesn't get it all,
Doesn't get one half either,
It all goes down, sing hup fol-de-rol la la

—"Helan går"

One of the nice things about *skål*, apart from its use as a toast, is that all Scandinavian languages say the same thing. Norwegian and Danish keep it as it appears, while the only difference in Icelandic and Faroese (spoken on the Faroe Islands in the Norwegian Sea) is the accent over the *a*, which changes to *á*. English transliterates the word into "skaal," and if you go back a thousand years, you can find *skál* in Old Norse: it means "bowl."

While the Vikings passed this heirloom down century after century, there isn't much more we know about medieval drinking traditions apart from that celebrations were boisterous and, as throughout the medieval world, ale was preferred to mead. Ale (from Old English *ealu*) enjoyed quite a different reputation then than it does now. High in calories, thought to be vastly more nutritious than water (it probably was), and palatable, ale was the medieval staple right up until beer stole the show in the sixteenth century.

Picture the United States' relationships with its many snacks—coffee, yogurt, nuts, cereal, McDonald's—and you'll get an idea of just how popular a *skál af öl* could be. In fact, for many centuries a bowl of ale was a standard breakfast—often mixed with nutmeg, sugar, egg whites, and brandy. Come to think of it, that "was" doesn't tell the whole story. Like it or not, according to articles in the *Los Angeles Times*, *Esquire*, and *Beer Magazine*, breakfast brews are on the rise. Mead (Old English *meodu*, meaning "honey") mainly survives in some craft mead recipes and in the legacy of boozy warlords and drunk peasants from medieval literature.

TASTING NOTE
brännvin
liqueur,
Absolut vodka.

Both beverages are drunk in Sweden, but neither plays as pivotal a role as spirits. One in particular is glorified more than the others: this is *brännvin* (literally "burning wine"), a type of crude vodka flavored with natural herbs. Swedes take a similar pride in their brännvin as craft brewers in their beers, and there are small distilleries all across the country where you can sample sundry brännvin to your heart's content.

Brännvin is only one of many Swedish drinking customs, which also include a literal toast to be eaten with toasts (appropriately, *skålat*) and a tradition of *snapsvisor*—songs sung on holidays to accompany toasting. The most popular is "Helan Går" (the ditty above). Charming as it is, snapsvisor can quickly enter the realm of the weird, such as with the raucous "Hej Tomtegubbar." Tomtegubbar, also Timtenisse or just Nisse, is a fractious garden gnome who comes out during winter holidays to scold naughty children and farmers for bad decorum like swearing, breaking glasses, or being rude to animals. Possessing gnome superstrength, Nisse punishes his victims by delivering thrashings, stealing hay, killing cows, or eating their porridge. Although respected by all good Swedes, Nisse is the subject of taunt rather than praise in this snapsvisor: "Hej, tomtegubbar, slå i glasen och låt oss lustiga vara!" ("Hey, Nisse, let's smash some glasses and have a good time!")

127

TURKISH

"Şerefe"
(sher'efe)

("Honor")

Linguistic terminology is home
to some of language's most colorful
words. Everyone who's ever asked for
a cup of "wa'er" knows what it means
to "glottalise." Other notables are
"bilabials," which is linguist for your
p's and *b*'s and *m*'s, and "plosive,"
or a little explosion of air as when
someone aggressively chants the
words "powder puff." There's
also the wonderful term
"agglutinization," which
literally means
"to glue to."

We probably all think of something different when we think of a gluey language. I imagine a Russian scraping off a long *nyeet* the way you would a dollop of peanut butter. Actually, gluey refers to the phenomenon of words to pick up sundry scraps of grammar. Witness the Turkish word for Europe: *Avrupa*. European? *Avrupalı*. To become European: *Avrupalılaş*. To cause to become European: *Avrupalılaştır*. Now, just watch what happens when we go a little further. Here's: "Of the ones that are ours that were unable to become Europeanized," *Avrupalılaştıramadıklarımızdan*. Finally, we come to this unwieldy humdinger: *Avrupalılaştıramadıklarımızdanmış-sınızcasına*, with the tidy definition of "as if you were reportedly of ours that were unable to be Europeanized," or "Hey, aren't you the son who couldn't get his German visa?"

Appropriate to Turkish's history, gluey also suggests staying power. Well before the Seljuks and Ottomans took it up and gave it the ride of a millennium, Turkish was enjoying a fine career mixing, mingling, and fighting with the crème de la crème of Eurasian warlords. From the third to the fifth centuries, it kicked at the Chinese and North India until, in 451, it graduated from petty mischief to full-scale slaughter when it saddled up with Attila the Hun. That would be a career bloody enough for any language's lifetime, but Turkish topped its own record when it flooded the cavalry of Genghis Khan in the twelfth and thirteenth centuries and ransacked just about everyone worth ransacking.

TASTING NOTE
rakı anise-flavored liqueur, Aryan yogurt beverage, chai, coffee.

Throughout this time, it retained a reputation for extra stickiness. Neither the rise of Arabic-speaking Muslims, its friends in Central Asia, nor the Soviet superpower could scrape the language off. In fact, Russia had every right to worry about the Turkish influence. With the single exception of Tajikistan, every country east of the Caspian Sea (and one west, Azerbaijan) in the former Soviet Union spoke a Turkic language. There's also a sizeable one, Uyghur, in the Xinjiang region of northwest China.

The Turkish toast *şerefe* descends from the Arabic *sharafan* and means "honor." Despite proximity to Bulgaria, Greece, and Armenia, casual drinking is not a big part of Turkey's mostly Islamic population. *Şerefe* is brought out primarily for special occasions. Nevertheless, drinking is ingrained in Turkey's heritage, and travelers who wish to savor a real Turkish drinking experience should visit a *meyhane*—a traditional Turkish restaurant first established during the time of the Byzantine Empire—and order a *tek* of *rakı*, an anise-flavored spirit mixed with water and served in champagne flutes.

32

UKRAINIAN

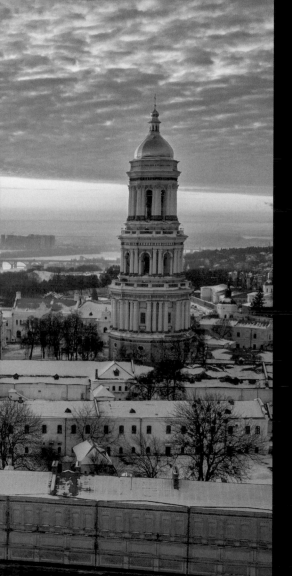

"Будьмо"
(bood'mo)

("We will")

Why do we have middle names? Why do men have nipples? Because why shouldn't we? There's a kind of symmetrical dignity in good middle names, whether it's the *D* in John D. Rockefeller, or the tunefulness of John Jacob Jingleheimer Schmidt.

In fact, we're so used to our nonsensical system we forget that middle names in the rest of the world still serve a very practical function, as anyone who's ever read a Russian novel will know.

Ukrainian middle names are called patronymics because they are made of the father's name plus a gender identifier. For girls it's *-ivna* or *-yivna*, and for boys it's *-ovych* or *-yovych*. If my daughter's name is Brenda, she is Brenda Brandonivna. If I name my son after me—and for some reason Russians and Ukrainians love doing this—he'll be Brandon Brandonovych. Generally, however, I'd just give my first and last name, which looks like a first name, plus an ending like *-chuk*. If my ancestors were also Brandons, then in very formal occasions, my son becomes Brandon Brandonovych Brandonchuk, and my daughter, Brenda Brandonivna Brandonchuk. Patronymics are used more often than we'd expect. If you visit Ukraine, you may find yourself at a Ukrainian dinner party juggling *-ivnas* and *-ovychs* like flaming torches.

Ukrainian is the language of chicken Kiev, *vareniki* dumplings, and *solyanka* (spicy soup), so dinner gatherings are something you can count on if you have Ukrainian friends. But pay attention because there are quite a few more rules of etiquette to follow. If you go to a dinner, you'll want to bring a bouquet of something. Flowers have their associations as gemstones do, but the main thing is to bring an odd number of them: I learned the difficult way that even-numbered bouquets symbolize mourning. When you get to the home, you must take off your shoes and then cross the threshold before shaking the hands of your host, if male, or offering a kiss, if female. Even if you're in an especially good mood, refrain from whistling indoors, or else you'll be warned that your money will fly away. When you sit down, do not offer to help the host manage with the alcohol. The host always pours and always uses the same hand for the job.

As for toasts, there's a three-pronged approach to new meetings, to new friends, and to women, and there's also the simple *bood'mo*, ("We will," from the phrase "we will live forever"). However, short toasts are seldom satisfactory. For a truly good cheers, you must stand, raise your glass, and offer a short anecdote summarizing why we toast to what we are about to toast. No clink afterward: just raise and down. You'll also probably take vodka shots sometime during the ceremonies, if not store bought then something brewed up by your host. This is *samohonka* (literally, "self-made"), and it packs a sly punch.

If you don't drink, saying "I don't drink" will offend your host, who'll think there's something at fault with his hospitality. Deferring requires a better excuse, such as a bad liver, a perpetual vow of abstinence, or pregnancy. If you're in the city, however, *bood'mo* will work just fine. It'll probably be accompanied by a shot of vodka, called a *horilka*.

33

WELSH

"Iechyd da"
(yeh'heed da)

("Good health")

You dwell in the Atlantic Ocean. Your life is a continuous struggle against the waters and the elements, but this is no trouble for you because you are a mighty beast, enormous and awesome to behold. Ruthlessly hunted by powerful enemies for much of your history, endangered, but never overcome. No one understands it outside your immediate domain, but those who have studied it draw attention to its strange, haunting rhythm and singsong quality.

Now, are you Welsh, or are you a whale? Because this chapter is entitled "Welsh," I'll assume nobody got that question wrong. And by the way, if you don't believe that part about living in the Atlantic Ocean, consider spending an autumn in Aberystwyth.

As for being an enormous beast, allow me to present Llanfairpwllgwyngyllgogerychwyrndrob-wllllantysiliogogogoch. (Translation: "St. Mary's Church in the hollow of the white hazel near a rapid whirlpool and the church of St. Tysilio of the Red Cave.") That's a small town on the island of Anglesey and the second largest one-word place name in the world. (First place goes to the Maoris.) Tourists take buses out just to get a picture with the railroad sign, and proud Welsh speakers tote the term around and spring it on unsuspecting listeners, like a long and colorful handkerchief. If you can say it in one breath, your Welsh friends might even stand you a pint.

Giant words aside, Welsh might also be responsible for some of the most peculiar aspects of English grammar, a case elegantly argued in linguist John McWhorter's book, *Our Magnificent Bastard Tongue*. These aspects are twofold: one is the interrogative *Do* form, and the other is the continuous, or progressive, aspect. Here's the gist of it: You see a friend. He is writing. You say, "Do you want to go eat?" He says, "Nope. I'm writing." Now, a vast amount of other language has it like this: "Want you to go eat?" And his reply: "Nope. I write." Not English and not Welsh.

The argument here is that while the sixth-century Anglo-Saxon invaders were kicking back in the country they'd just wrested from the Romans, the Celtic Britons were forced into the corners of the country but went on pushing their own grammar into the language of their neighbors with the pointy end of the teacher stick. The eventual compromise that came from these languages, primarily Germanic Anglo-Saxon and Celtic, was a hybrid now called Old English or Anglo-Saxon.

But most of us don't think of obscure parts of grammar when we think of Welsh. We think of Dylan Thomas, corgis, and good winter flannel. *Corgi* and *flannel* are both Welsh words, by the way, and there's another—*penguin*—that is up for debate. There are no penguins in Wales of course—the penguin in Welsh refers to the flightless great auk who loves a cold coastal climate almost as much as any patriotic Seattleite.

Welsh, Cymraeg (*cum'raig*), is spoken by about 560,000 people: not much on a global scale but not bad for a language with two thousand years of conquerors putting it down. It's a miracle there's so much Welsh left at all.

Iechyd da (good health) is a standard affair, with smiles and clinking glasses. Ales and ciders are traditionally the way to go, and for a truly kitschy experience, don't forget to raise a pint to that most famous of Welsh kings, Arthur of the Britons.

PART TWO

EURASIA

"Կենացը"
(kenat'sy)

("Life")

Lift a glass with the Armenian *kenat'sy*, and you'll be taking things a step further than in most countries. Unlike many European toasts, *kenat'sy* doesn't come from a word meaning "happiness" but from the word *k'yank*, meaning "life"—similar in spirit to the Hebrew *l'chaim*. "To life" plus a clink and a drink of beer, spirits, or wine.

142

34

ARMENIAN

Even if you're not much of a drinker, if you're a newcomer to Armenia, you'd be remiss not to sample the local specialties. First up are the sweet red wines. You'll have plenty of choices: grapes have been cultivated in the regions of Armenia at least since 4100 BC, and there are dozens of present-day wineries. A typical flavor is sweet, dry, sherryesque, but that certainly isn't a rule set in stone. Armas Estates features a shimmering cast of award-winning wines, from dry reds, rosés, white semisweets, and something called "golden berry," which literally looks like a bottle filled with molten metal. If that doesn't wet your whistle, a sip of Armenia's world-famous cognac might do the trick. The spirit takes its name from Mount Ararat, the same mountain where Noah docked his ark after his tumultuous sea voyage, after which the aged patriarch then proceeded to plant the world's first vineyards.

Now comes the toast. This can be a simple *kenat'sy* or a complex affair, depending on your table's MC. In Armenian, the word for the job is *t'amada*, and the job is quite the professional task. Tamadas are the heads of the table during celebrations, but more than simply calling the shots, it's their task to compose the spirit of the table and the rhythm of the drinking. This can be done in a variety of forms, all of which involve professional showmanship and awarding toasts. "Sing, recite poetry, have a talent of beautiful rhetoric, this is what a tamada must be rich with," says the reporter Gurgen Stepanyan. A tamada is a professional partyer plus a safekeeper of cultural tradition and prestige, and as such, his or her position is revered: the word means not just head of the table but manager and coordinator. In this, the tamada is a one-man party, taking his inspiration from the traditions of the masters of ceremony who first raised toasts during the symposiums of ancient Greece. It's no small wonder that masters of the position are in such high demand.

35

AZERBAIJANI

"Sağlığ"
(saa'glick)

("To your health")

Divide and conquer. Turkmen and Turkish. Gagauz and Turkish. Azeri and Turkish. Northern Azeri and Southern Azeri. Azeri Turkish and Turkish. Istanbul Turkish and Turkish. What's the difference between all these languages aside from their names?

TASTING NOTE
Xirdalan lager
beers, wine in
the north-central
region around
Baku and
İsmayıllı.

The short answer is that there aren't very many—discounting the differences in dialect, loanwords, and separate scripts— but like so much in language, this all depends on who you talk to.

Some Azerbaijani consider the language to be as close to Turkish as American to British English, while according to a recent study, the language was only about 60 percent mutually intelligible with Turkish. Culture certainly plays a significant factor in the matter as well, and many Azerbaijanis watch Turkish soap operas and send their children to Turkish-speaking schools. To further complicate matters, Azeri is also split into two dialects, a northern one, spoken in Azerbaijan, and a southern one, spoken in Iran. Northern Azeri is written in Latin script and has more Russian influences, as well as a pattern of stress that modifies it slightly from Istanbul Turkish. Southern Azeri is spoken in northern Iran and uses the Persian alphabet. It also has more Persian loanwords, plus an ongoing dispute with Iran over a hunk of its land, but here isn't the place to get into any of that.

Scripts and loanwords aside, both languages are still highly mutually intelligible, and it would appear the greatest differentiating factor in the whole language stew is history—specifically, a history of movement. Much of this happened during the Turkic migration of the sixth to eleventh centuries, some more during the 1990s, all the way to today, when more than sixteen million Azeris are living outside Azerbaijan. But that's enough of numbers— it's time to talk wines.

The regions of ancient Azerbaijan have long enjoyed a flourishing viticulture—one that even found mention in the pages of Herodotus in the fifth century BC and in Strabo five hundred years later. In fact, it's estimated that Azeri wine making dates to 4000 BC; however, illustrious history didn't seem to matter much when it came to Soviet prohibition. Since Azerbaijan gained independence in 1991, Azeri wine grapes have been reforging a name for themselves with steadily increasing rates of production and quality recognition. Sweet reds are in much esteem, as in Armenia, but if you look hard enough, you'll find a few good dry reds as well. Azerbaijanis drink about 10 million liters a year, which doesn't sound like much (Georgia drinks 95 million) until you consider how wine only just made it back in the game (the largest winery, Vinagro, was established in 2006), and also if you consider the fact that over 90 percent of the population is Muslim, or dry—at least, ostensibly. The most common toast is *sağlığ* (to your health), but the Turkish *şerefe* is also used. Although generally reserved for more formal occasions, such as weddings or birthday parties, *sağlığ* can also be brought out for simple toasts as well.

36

BELARUSIAN

"На здароўе"
(na zdaroye)
("To health")

How much difference could there be between Russian and a language that literally calls itself "White Russian"? You'd be surprised. In fact, if you go and find yourself a Ukrainian, a Belarusian, and a Russian and sit them down next to each other, the Belarusian and Ukrainian would understand approximately 75 percent of each other's language, whereas the frustrated Russian, catching about 50 percent, would be banging his head against the table.

151

What accounts for this mysterious Ukrainian/Belarusian partnership? In the thirteenth and fourteenth centuries, Belarus was subsumed into the Grand Duchy of Lithuania—a massive European state that comprised territories of modern Ukraine, Poland, and Lithuania. A little more than a century after the seizure of Belarus, Lithuania's grand duke married the queen of Poland and was then able to add the fancy new kingdom to an already big collection. The eventual effects of this Polish-Lithuanian (but mostly Polish) Commonwealth were positive at least until the empire went belly up. Certainly though, the amount of religious and linguistic tolerance granted to Yiddish-speaking Jews, Islamic Tatars, and various sects of Christianity (Protestantism, Eastern Orthodoxy) was liberal even by today's standards. In fact, by the sixteenth century, democratic principles of tolerance and equal rights had led to the development of the political system "Golden Liberty," whose fundamental principle is summarized in the Polish proverb "Szlachcic na zagrodzie równy wojewodzie" ("The tenant farmer noble on his estate is equal to the warlord"). That's a lovely way to sort of democratize some of the privileged population, but it was revolutionary in Golden Liberty times. The territories of Belarus and the Belarusian language—which like all eastern Slavic languages was then referred to as Ruthenian—enjoyed many of these benefits right up until in the eighteenth- and nineteenth-century invasions by Cossack rebels, Swedes, and Turks destroyed the commonwealth for good.

Belarus and its fledgling language, which had been replaced by Polish in 1696, were quickly swept up by Catherine the Great and partitioned, and a new era of subordination began. Polonization changed to

Russification, and Belarusian, which was just beginning to be spoken again, was promptly banned. And from there things only got worse.

A 1918 attempt to create a Belarusian People's Republic in lands occupied by World War I–era Germany lasted for less than a year. Following this, Belarus was again divided, this time between Poland and the Soviet Union, under whose heel it would remain until it declared its independence in 1990—this time, hopefully, for good. Unfortunately, a severely fraught history, fractured identity, and the highest alcohol consumption rates in the world (17.5 liters of alcohol consumption per capita, compared with the world average of 6.2 liters) pose huge challenges for an independent state without resources, but Belarusians are willing to do whatever their newly reclaimed country requires.

As in other Slavic languages, you generally offer a toast to something aside from just health: *na zdaroye*. Health is good the first time around, but a good second would be to friendship: *droozhboo*. The third as a rule should fall on love: *kach'annie*. You'll find plenty of vodka, but Belarus offers something else special and a lot more dangerous, under the forbidding name *krambambula*. What puts the "bam" in krambambula is the liquor cocktail that goes into it: gin, vodka, or rum (maybe all three), plus red wine. That's one option, but another version of the krambam involves vodka plus honey and spices: the taste is reportedly of mead, or a cool mulled wine. Much more manageable.

TASTING NOTE
Zubrovka vodka, krambambula, kvass rye beer.

153

37

GEORGIAN

"გაუმარჯოს"
(gua'marjos)

("Long life")

Georgia takes its alcohol seriously, and it's not hard imagining why. After all, there's a reputation for hearty wine drinkers to consider, beginning somewhere around 6000 BC (the date ascribed to an ancient Georgian drinking horn) and continuing up to our modern day. Is Georgia's wine the oldest in the world? It would appear so, but the facts are never all that simple.

An Armenian would never dream of handing king grape over to their neighbors in the north; nor would Persia, Bulgaria, or Greece. There's archaeological evidence of wine residue more than 6,000 years old found in the region of modern-day Armenia, but more famous is the story of Noah, who, already well past half a millennium, cultivated the world's first vintage and then, to celebrate, embarked on the world's first binger (with disastrous results).

Regardless of where the wine lies, a good toast is short to follow, and Georgia has the art of the toast down pat. There's a story told among Georgians that when God was creating the world, he summoned all peoples to come to him, so he could divide the land among them. The Georgians were characteristically late, and when they arrived at the meeting, they were informed that all the land had already been divided up. "We're sorry we're late," they replied, "but we were busy drinking to you." Flattered, God awards them the hunk of land he'd been reserving for himself, and this of course was Georgia.

Now, regarding these toasts, Georgia and Armenia both share the tradition of the tamada, or toastmaster, whose job in an informal setting is to organize toasts and, in formal occasions, to act as drinking MC. Drinking and toasting occasions are called *supras* (from the Georgian word for "tablecloth"), and there is a loose format to them. First toasts are generally to peace, while the second and third are usually to Georgia, to the recently departed, to God, to giving thanks, and so on. After that it's fair game. What follows could be a ten-second quip or a five-minute speech extolling anything from love, friendship, and good weather to a great new deal on a used car. (Possible, if unlikely: good toasts are judged in either laughs, tears, or hear-hears!) Each of these is accompanied by a *guamarjos* (from *gamarj'veba*, meaning "to victory"), used as a ritual salute for ancient Georgians going off to war.

This is followed by a big swig, but never of beer. In the heart of wine country, a brew probably isn't what you're looking for anyway. Wine is the ruby standard, followed by brandy, then cordial. Toasting with beer is considered an insult. If spirit is what you're after, you can't go wrong with *chacha*—grappa, sometimes called moonshine or vine vodka, brewed from a variety of fruits and herbs, like figs, oranges, mulberries, or tangerines.

Finally, a "glass" of something might not give you the right idea. Georgians have traditionally taken their alcohol either from bowls or horns—called *kantsi*—a bit like the Anglo-Saxons of *Beowulf*. To really feel like a Georgian, a nice drinking horn might be just what you're looking for.

38

KAZAKH

"Ал ендеше қағысайық"
(al endeshe kagy'saikh)

("Let's raise a glass")

Kazakhs take enormous pride in their national traditions as well as in their friendly hospitality, claims which are entirely justified. Like in ancient Greece, guest reception plays a huge role in Kazakh culture, and the language reflects the many different customs travelers can expect.

159

TASTING NOTE
kumiss
(fermented
mare's milk),
Snow Queen
vodka,
chai.

And as we're on the subject of expectations, it might as well be known that Borat-related jokes probably aren't the best way to impress your Kazakh compatriots. As for this guest/host vocabulary, for starters there is *konakasy*, a name that refers to the rich traditional cuisine set out for newcomers.

"Guest" is a tricky word, and Kazakh employs three words for the job: *arnayy konak* (special invitee), *kudayy konak* (random stranger), and *kydyrma konak* (unexpected guest), all of whom will be offered the rich konakasy hospitality. After several plates, the host may then raise a glass of *kymyz* (also called *kumis*, fermented mare's milk similar to kefir) with the words *al endeshe kagysaikh* (let's raise a glass) or *Dosymyzdyn koormetyne alyp koyayk* (let's raise a glass for our friend). Once you've had your drink, you'll be expected to offer praise, the ritual response being *bal siyakti*, meaning "sweet as honey." There are then the national dishes, *zhal* (smoked horse neck lard) and *quyrdak* (a mélange of horse, sheep, and cow heart, liver, and kidney, among other various innards), and the succulent *qazy*. Mouthwatering to some and unwholesome to others, qazy is horse rib meat and horse butt, sliced, smoked, and salted. This might be accompanied by a dish of boiled horse meat and noodles, called *beshbarmak*, and if you're celebrating something special, the table may also be adorned with a lamb's head. Once you've had your fill and downed a few glasses of kymyz or vodka, the host may then exercise his

right (*konakkade*) to request his guest to perform some kind of entertainment, whether reciting poetry, playing a musical instrument, dancing, juggling, backflipping (this has fallen rather out of vogue), and so on. The party may then continue to make merry and raise many more toasts: visitors would be wise to prepare for a long night!

"Эрүүл мэндийн төлөө"
(er'ool men'deen too'loo)

("For health")

There is a famous story told about Mongolia in the sixteenth and seventeenth centuries that takes place between the powerful Mongolian state (Northern Yuan Dynasty) and the Manchus—an ethnic group that used to control a large part of northeast Asia.

39
MONGOLIAN

In the story, one of these young lords, Yadam, is summoned to the court of the Manchus for an honorary banquet, where he is served a bowl of a ceremonious beverage. Dipping his ring finger into the bowl to give the customary toast—"for the eternal heaven, for the earth, and for our people"—some of the liquid drips onto his wedding ring. The ring begins to corrode, and Yadam, seeing that the dishes have been poisoned, is able to warn his comrades. Mongolians today still give the same blessing and dip with the same finger, appropriately dubbed the "Yadam."

Urbanization, globalization, modernization have come to dominate, but at the same time many of the bedrocks in culture, life, and ritual remain largely unchanged in Mongolian society. About 26 percent of the population (as of 2015) still live as nomads schlepping their yurts across the steppe. Many families still make a ritual offering of fresh milk twice a day to the gods, and the "five-headed cattle" (in Mongolian, *tavan khoshuu mal*) of goats, sheep, camels, cows/yaks, and horses is still the bulwark of the Mongolian economy, although horses occupy the place of highest importance. It was the horse, after all, that allowed Genghis Khan to flesh out the largest contiguous land empire in the world, and it is the horse that guarantees transport and provisions for the nomad.

Fermented milk, whether from a camel or mare, is called *airag*, and serves as the Mongolian national beverage. The popularity of airag is best expressed in the saying "without airag, there is no summer." Fermented milk produces a commonly consumed and popular alcohol called *shimiin arkhi*—Mongolian milk vodka. And if you sift the remaining milk mash, you'll end up with dried curds, a dish called *aaruul*.

Finally, a note about that funky alphabet. Yes, that is a thousand-year-old alphabet, the only up-down, left-to-right alphabet still in active use. And yes, some Mongolians—not all—still write like this. They are generally found in Inner Mongolia, an autonomous region of China between its northern border and Mongolia's southern border. The alphabet was used throughout Mongolia until the adoption of Cyrillic during the communist era, and, like English and its armies of silent *gh*'s and its shapeshifting *ough*, it's still holding on to much of its outdated spelling conventions. Throughout its past, Mongolian has been rudely forced into Cyrillic script and even Chinese characters. Antique though the Mongolian writing system might be, it is a source of justifiable pride and unlikely to diminish any time soon.

"Барои Саломати"
(bar'ee saloma'tee)

("To health")

How do we get to the bottom of a country known as the "Roof of the World"? Comparing Tajik's toast to the Persian toast gives plenty of information straight off the bat. Tajik and Persian are the same minus the obvious difference of the alphabet.

40

TAJIK

TASTING NOTE
Alcohol is
discouraged by
many, but there
are local beers
and spirits, like
Tajikistan vodka,
green and black
tea, and fruit
sherbets.

Dari Persian, the national language of Afghanistan, also falls into this group of near-identical Persian dialects and only operates under a different name for political reasons.

Persia exported an eastern dialect of its language after Cyrus the Great of Persia conquered the Sogdian state (modern Tajikistan and Uzbekistan). However, saying that Sogdian was conquered by the Persians doesn't really give the right idea. During its lifetime, these Sogdian territories were never politically unified, and even while the territory changed hands, Sogdians exercised their influence in other ways aside from the political, some of these spheres quite high indeed. Alexander the Great's wife Roxana was a Sogdian (and responsible for having the king's other two wives murdered), and so was Spitamenes, a warlord who mounted an uprising against him.

But more important than murderers and rebels were the Sogdian contributions of the cities Bukhara and Samarkand. Still standing even after five millennia, Samarkand was the central hub for traders during the time of the Silk Road—the most significant trade and information highway until the internet.

Sometime after the rebellion of the Sogdian general An Lushan, which effectively ended the Chinese Tang dynasty, the Chinese emperor outlawed Sogdians and Sogdian religions, which, at that time, included Zoroastrianism, Manichaeism, Christianity, and Buddhism (the law against

Buddhism clearly didn't last). Inversely, as Sogdian civilization and culture declined with the Tang, the Iranian Samanid Empire rose, and with it came a renewed interest in Persian arts and language—the language that would inspire modern Tajik. The Samanid Empire was also responsible for restoring the enlarged cities of Samarkand and Bukhara back to Persian control—a reason why Tajiks claim Samanid as the first Tajik state.

If you're following any of this on a map, you've probably noticed the inconsistency in referencing Samarkand and Bukhara in an article about Tajikistan, as both these cities are located in Uzbekistan. To understand how this happened requires a jump ahead to the 1920s and an introduction to the acronym NTD (National Territorial Delimitation). Inaugurated by the new USSR, this process, still contentious to this day, drew thousands of miles or border between a host of newly minted Soviet republics, or autonomous Soviet republics, among them Tajikistan and Uzbekistan. With the NTD boundaries drawn, both Bukhara and Samarkand slipped beyond Tajikistan's boundaries, Samarkand by just forty kilometers.

Tajikistan was declared a Soviet Socialist Republic in 1929, and with the disintegration of the Soviet Union in 1991, the state rather reluctantly declared full independence. The declaration sparked a bitter civil war, which led to a mass exodus to Afghanistan and internal problems that persist to this day. Thus, the illustrious beginnings of this region have devolved into strife: a tough change for a once affluent region.

Despite its large Muslim population, there is and has been casual drinking in Tajikistan at least since the Middle Ages, where patrons could frequent a *kharobot* or *maykhona*, a kind of medieval bar. For an innocent and law-abiding social activity, travelers can take part in a traditional tea ceremony during which the host serves guests in special cups called *piyola*, filling them only halfway: a full teacup implies that the host wants the guest to drink and leave sooner. Teacups may then be raised and a toast given, either *baroi salomati* or *salomat boshem* (to health).

As for alcohol, drinking is common, although rigid Tajik laws ensure that much of it be done in secret. And should you choose to indulge anything so frivolous and merry as, say, a birthday party, be certain to lock your doors, bar your windows, and turn off all cameras: Tajik law strictly forbids them.

41

UZBEK

"Sog'liq uchun"
(sog'lik uch'un)

("Health")

The Eurasian steppe has been home, hunting grounds, battlefield, and graveyard to
some of history's most feared warlords.
An Atilla is bad enough, but when the
place is supplemented with a Genghis
Khan/Khan dynasty and then a Tamer-
lane, and when the various fighting
factions only come to heel when the
Russian Empire mounts an enormous
conquest, then the Eurasian steppe
sounds like a likely candidate
for most dangerous
place in history.

173

Not only are the steppes the scene of some of the most brutal conquests over the past thousand years, but they proved ultimately too vast and too slippery for any one ruler to keep a hold on.

This is not true for the language, however, which in all Central Asian countries, apart from Tajikistan, is a variety of Turkic. Turkic languages have an enormous following, not always easy to pick out unless you know where to look. There are the Central Asian countries Kyrgyzstan, Uzbekistan, Turkmenistan, and Kazakhstan, where nomadic Turkic tribes settled during the time of the Turkic migration between the sixth and eleventh centuries, when most of the area was known as Transoxania. Around the year 840, part of the Uyghur Turkic Empire spread into Mongolia but was later pushed out by the Kyrgyz into the region known now as Xinjiang ("western frontier"—and the Uyghur language has its own word for "cheers" by the way: *hoshe*). Around the same time, the Turkish language also bridged the Siberian plateau and scattered a number of dialects all over the place, including a couple—Sakha and Dolgan—as far north as Yakutsk. We are now in far north Siberia, quite a long way from Uzbekistan and from our original purpose, which is toasts.

Uzbekistan is a Muslim-dominated country with a surprisingly lax drinking culture. During celebrations, vodka is chugged out of porcelain bowls to the accompaniment of spirited toasts and speeches (*nutq so'zlab qadah ko'tarish*, "a speech and a toast") and the occasional, one-word toast *sog'liq uchun* (health). If the occasion isn't quite so formal, the simpler "long life" will do: *yashasin*. As was mentioned, you'll probably find plenty of vodka, and you might occasionally encounter a fizzy grain beverage of very low alcohol called *boza*, although this is more common among Kazakhs, Kyrgyz, and in Turkey, where it comes flavored with cinnamon and roasted chickpeas.

For regular nights out, most Uzbeks would prefer green tea (*ko'k choy*), black tea (*qora choy*), or tea with sugar (*shirin choy*): all are popular. If you have the honor of being hosted by an Uzbek family, you might be seated down and have your tea poured from a *piyola*, a special porcelain bowl. Tradition states that the tea is poured from the teapot (*choynak*) into the bowl and back three times before it is suitable for drinking, at which point the guest will then be served first.

PART THREE

ASIA AND AUSTRONESIA

42

BURMESE

(Myanmar)

"ချကွ"
(cha kwa)
("Let's hit it")

When I think of temples, I imagine more of the ruined Indiana Jones kind than the ones you usually see in China or India bursting with pagodas and stupas. But to everyone their own preference. There certainly isn't any shortage of varieties.

179

The Sri Harmandir Sahib temple in Indian Punjab—the most important pilgrimage site for Sikh Muslims—is made of solid gold; the Athenian Temple of Hephaestus, of Doric columns. The Egyptian Karnak is called a temple, but here the term is an umbrella word designating a whole village of sandstone pylons, sculptures, chapels, statues, courtyards, obelisks, and miniature houses of worship. The Bahá'í Lotus Temple in Delhi is made of nine enormous marble slabs shaped like an opening lotus flower. Pashupatinath Temple in Kathmandu carries out live cremations, and Karni Mata temple in Rajasthan is infested with rats. Jews refer to their place of worship as a temple as do Mormons, Freemasons, and Orthodox Christians, and Western Christianity has its fair share of temples in Spain, France, Poland, and Mexico.

In Hungarian, the word for "church" is *templom*, and in medieval Irish, *teampall*. As a matter of fact, temple comes from Latin *templum*, meaning simply an "open, consecrated space." I mention all of this simply to illustrate that temple mania is a worldwide phenomenon, not confined to the more popular locations in Cambodia, Indonesia, and India.

To get a truly awe-inspiring temple experience, travelers should consider dropping by Myanmar, specifically Bagan (sometimes Pagan). Thousands of egg- and bell-shaped pagodas cover the hills, many of which have been standing for over a millennium, in spite of the earthquake in 2016, and the sheer number and artistry of the temples make the landscape comparable to Angkor Wat.

Myanmar has had and still has a fraught and complex history, but tourism is on the rise. Myanmars are generally thrilled for the chance to greet Westerners and will be happy to raise toasts with the English "cheers," but you'll be quite popular if you can salute with the Burmese *cha kwa*—meaning "let's hit it."

TASTING NOTE
Myanmar rum,
Pegu Club
cocktail,
domestic
lager beers.

Buddhists generally don't drink, but it doesn't at all follow that the country is dry. As a matter of fact, one of the country's most enduring landmarks, aside from its temples, is the famous Rangoon Pegu Club. Built in the 1880s, this most famous of gentlemen's clubs catered to the British military elite up until the end of colonial rule. Its status has declined, but the club is still famous with tourists and known to cocktail lovers as the original home of the Pegu Club gin cocktail.

Nevertheless, if there's a Burmese drinking staple, it wouldn't be cocktails but green tea, which is so popular that it doubles down as both beverage and national dish. *Lahpet thoke* is a pickled green tea salad enjoyed throughout Myanmar as a onetime delicacy but now as snack, entrée, and dessert. When you sit down, you'll probably be invited to *tone saung par own*, the ritual words used by hosts to let guests know it's OK to start chowing down.

43

CEBUANO

"Kanpai"
(kan'pie)

("Dry glass")

Mountains and islands tend to do similar things to languages. No, they don't smash them up. Their function is more like a refrigerator, and what's preserved is dialects. As a rule, they precede the language until an enormously patient scholar swoops in, cooks them up, and serves them nice and standardized.

This is the story of literally every language we know. But more often than not, dialects stay dialects—that is, they stay languages that just haven't yet been sorted into more inclusive wholes.

Southeast Asia is home to the most linguistically diverse countries on the planet. New Guinea is number one with over 850, and Indonesia is a close second with 700. The Philippines are down the list a little way—180—but with differences comparable to those between many European languages. For example, there is Chavacano (meaning "vulgar"), a Spanish-based creole (the only Spanish creole in Asia) developed during the time of the Spanish-American War. The Filipino proverb "He who doesn't look back won't reach his destination" in Chavacano looks like this: "Quien no ta bira cara na su origen no de incarsa na su destinacion." On the island Basilan, where Yakan is acknowledged to be the native language, the proverb goes "Mang gey matau mamayam si bakas palaihan nen, gey tekka si papilihan nen." Finally, just to add extra confusion, each of the island's immigrant populations go on speaking their native languages, which include Arabic, Persian, a Taiwanese dialect, and Cebuano. All this on an island about as big as Phoenix, Arizona.

The northern province of Cebu does a similar juggling feat, but on a much smaller scale. The Cebuano language has taken such prominence that it's referred to simply as Bisaya, a reference to its status in the Visayan language group. This would be a bit like calling Italian "Romance." Cebu is one of the most prosperous regions in the country, and no travelers combing the Philippines will want to miss the region's stunning beaches or the beautiful cathedrals of its Spanish past.

As in Tagalog, residents drink and toast their *tagays* in the street, generally sharing one cup for a whole group. Depending on who you're drinking with, you might either get toasts (with no clinks) with the word *tagay* or with *kanpai*, a Japanese loanword meaning "bottoms up." If you're in a festive group, your party will chant "Kam pay! Kam pay!" until you take your shot, but you must be careful you don't take too long, or else someone may comment that *gilumut na nah imong baso oh*, which means "your glass has gone mossy" (from waiting too long).

44

CHINESE

(Mandarin)

干杯
(gān bēi)

("Dry glass")

Everyone knows that *gan bei* means "dry glass." The real question is this: aside from Tsingtao beer, what are you supposed to drink in China? That would be Moutai—sometimes "Mao-tai" in honor of the chairman—premium *baijiu*, or "white liquor," China's number one way to lift your spirits.

When Richard Nixon visited China in 1972, his dinner guest Zhou En-lai proudly informed the president that Moutai lubricated the Long March and was used by the communists to combat exhaustion and heal various wounds, virtues that prompted a toast from the US president. And two years later, when Deng Xiaoping was visiting the White House, Henry Kissinger expressed what whiskey drinkers have known for centuries: "I think if we drink enough Moutai, we can solve anything."

Actually, for the Chinese this isn't too far from the truth. Alcohol's first purpose in China has always been medicinal rather than recreational. A century ago, it wouldn't have been uncommon for apothecaries to help you treat minor aches and pains with a jar of snake wine, usually vivisected right before your eyes so that you'd know it was fresh. Most Chinese homes still keep a bottle of it handy somewhere, especially if you're in the southern regions.

But whatever special status Moutai has, Western dislike for the alcohol is at least as fervent as the praise. Although Moutai is the most valuable liquor company in the world, 95 percent of its sales are Chinese. Most

Americans have never even heard the word *baijiu*. The Chinese are quick to correct this atrocity when hosting Westerners, but Americans ought to be warned: for the uninitiated the bottle itself looks like and will probably taste like a bottle of paint thinner. Like pig brains, it's doubtful Moutai will ever become quite as large a presence in Western culture. At least, not in the spirit of chopsticks or pandas.

Thankfully, there's more than one way to cross the East/West palate gap, and this way is cassia wine. Made from a combination of weak baijiu and Osmanthus flowers, cassia wine is fragrant and sweet. Drink it when you like, but it's generally consumed at the Mid-Autumn Festival where it accompanies the exchange and eating of mooncakes: beautiful pastries filled with bean or seed paste. Each region has its specialty, but one of the tastiest—桂花酒, or *gui hua jiu*—can be found in scenic Guilin. But this is to be expected. The name of this florid city literally means "Osmanthus forest."

飲勝
(yám sing)

("Bottoms up")

有缘无缘 *(yu an, mo an,)*
大家来作伙 *(dagai lai zui hui)*
烧酒喝一杯 *(shuo jiu li din bei)*
乎干啦 *(ho da la!)*

Luck or not
Let's make friends anyway,
Drink the wine from the cup
And let it go dry!

—Hakka drinking song

190

45

CHINESE

(Dialects)

Ask anyone what the difference is between a dialect and a language, and you'll probably hear something about numbers of speakers or about accent, grammar, and spelling. Dialects sometimes get a bad rap when compared to the languages they service. In actuality, a language is nothing more than a dialect, or as the corny linguist's joke puts it, a dialect with an army and a navy.

This is certainly true of Mandarin. As the name suggests, Mandarin was historically the speech of the powerful, spoken in the courts in the southern capital, Nanjing (which was the capital three times, first in 1368 and finally in 1937), and also in the northern capital, Beijing (the capital from as early as 1421 and again from 1949 to the present day). The Chinese name for Mandarin, *pǔtōnghuà*, meaning "common speech," gives a rather inaccurate picture. First of all, Mandarin is not based on a standard of all China's collected dialects but only of some of the northern dialects, especially that of Beijing.

As for being the common form of Chinese, while 70 percent of the population speaks it, there are as many as 400 million Chinese who don't speak it well enough according to national standards. For these 400 million, the go-to language is a regional dialect. And what Chinese terms a dialect is much closer to what we could call a language. Take the Mandarin word for "man"—人, *rén* (that accent means the syllable is spoken with a rising tone). In Hokkien, the dialect of Fujian Province and in Singapore, the word is *jîn* (spoken with a rising and then falling tone).

In the most widely spoken dialect, Yue, or Cantonese of the southern provinces, you get *ján*.

What do all these dialect regions have in common when it comes to drinking? A love of noodles, spicy food, and some good drinking games. The most popular you'll encounter is played with cups of dice. Each player starts with a cup of five dice. Shake them around in the cup, and then take a look at your numbers without letting your partner see. After this, guess the total number of sides facing up between both sets of dice—for example, three fives or two sixes. The second guess must go higher than the first (five fives, four sixes). After the guesses, flip cups, and the loser drinks. In lieu of cups of dice, you can also press your luck with the finger-guessing game. It looks like rock paper scissors, only instead you lay down a combination of fingers while calling out what you think the total number of digits will be. If neither of you are correct, the game continues immediately and goes until one of you is accurate. Chinese drinking parties are loud, drunken, and full of games, so expect a wild and headache-inducing night if you're going out on the town.

"I ke ola"
(i kee ola)

("To life")

Mahalo for reading this chapter about Hawaii, and alooooooha. You're in the paradise of the Pacific, land of the luau, the hula, and the *humuhum-unukunukuapua'a*, literally "fish that grunts like a pig." It's no joke: this fish really *can* grunt, although you're probably going to need to shell out for a snorkeling lesson before you get the chance to hear it.

HAWAIIAN

But let's go back and take another look at that name.

As long words go, this one isn't all that bad, especially given the fact that almost everyone can already work their way around more difficult vowel clusters like those in lei, luau, Maui, and Hawaii. A syllable always ends with a vowel, and the inventory of consonants is just eight: the second lowest of any known language (the lowest being six). By way of comparison, English has twenty-four consonants (twenty-five if you're the kind of person who says "chutzpah"). All of which is to say that the scary snorting fish gets broken down as the quite manageable: hoo-moo-hoo-moo-noo-koo-noo-koo-ah-poo-ah-ah. Once you can say this three times fast, you're ready to move on to other vowel-centric wildlife. *Aeaea* (small green fish), *'iao*, *uoa*, and *uouoa* are all names for various fish, and *oau* is a cat. If you're out bird-watching, you might be lucky enough to catch sight of the *oioe* (Hawaiian tern) or the endangered *ou* (honeycreeper) and even hear his *oioioi* (chirp). You might hear other birdsongs as well, as they *oooo* (crow) and *oeoe* (whistle). Sadly, you will not see any wild *oo* (Kaua'i o'o), as the bird went extinct in 1987. If you'd like to listen to the oo song, a recording is available at the Cornell Lab of Ornithology, although you must be a *hooiaioia* (certified) member to gain access.

This is certainly more Hawaiian than the average tourist will ever encounter, but speaking Hawaiian wherever you can is a good idea for several reasons. Despite low numbers of native speakers, Hawaiian-language immersion schools (Pūnana Leo) are becoming more popular, and a surge of interest in Hawaiian studies has occasioned a Hawaiian culture renaissance. There's also the fact that the words are just plain fun to say, and that Hawaiians love when tourists use the language. A well-timed aloha, an invitation to grab a cocktail *pau hana* (at happy hour), or saying mahalo to a surf instructor for his *kokua* (help) will all buy you much more love than the same phrases in English.

TASTING NOTE
awa liquor,
mai tai
cocktail.

The same is also true for *i ke ola* (here's to life), which is more intimate than the English. To do the toast properly, lift your cocktail, look your companion in the eyes, pronounce his or her name, and then follow up with the Hawaiian i ke ola. Adding *maikai* or *pono* at the end of the blessing will also invoke feelings of goodness or excellence (*pono* means "righteousness").

As for particular alcohol, while Hawaiians may be the kings of cocktails, it is not rum or vodka that carries the most cultural significance but a liquor distilled from a root called *awa*. (In fact, that quintessential Hawaiian cocktail—the mai tai—takes its name from Tahitian.) Sometimes called kava depending on where you are, for thousands of years awa has been gulped down as ceremonial beverage, ingested as a headache reliever, and poured out as an offering to the dead. Among tourists, it is used as a muscle relaxant served in more ritualized settings, but awa is making a popular comeback at some bars and restaurants throughout the eight islands, generally among the college aged. In addition to boasting hundreds of years of cultural significance, awa drinking promises one additional benefit . . . no hangovers!

47

HINDI

एक जाम . . . के नाम
(ek jam _ ke naam)
("To the honor of . . .")

What's the deal with India's languages?
Twenty-two languages and thirteen
different scripts. Why can't a country
choose one and be done with it? There
are three big components to this question. One, Indian languages fall into two
very separate families, Indo-Aryan in the
north and Dravidian in the south (with
a small scattering of languages from
Austro-Asiatic and the Sino-Tibetan
families). Two, the collection of Indian states is similar to Europe, and
no one is seriously asking why
Europeans don't all speak
one common
European language.

199

And three, technically, there *was* an official language—Sanskrit. In fact, you could argue that Bengali, Gujarati, and Hindi are really vernacular forms of Sanskrit, in a similar way that French, Spanish, and Italian are dialects of Latin.

Sanskrit's career as a literary, as opposed to spoken, language also mirrors that of medieval Latin, although whereas Latin developed more verbal forms that made speaking progressively easier, Sanskrit was taken under the wing by a philologist called Panini, who tightened and disciplined its grammar. Furthermore, even from its mythologized beginnings, Sanskrit was seen as a language of enormous scriptural and liturgical importance.

In its earliest, or Vedic, phase, it birthed the enormous collection of Hindu religious poems known as the Rigveda. This ought to have been an achievement to outlast the lifetime of any language, but Sanskrit wasn't done. In its second stage, it bore two of the most astonishing mythological-philosophical epics world literature has ever seen: the Ramayana (twice the length of the combined *Iliad* and *Odyssey*) and the even longer Mahabharata. Breathing life into superfine poetic epics isn't something that Sanskrit alone can lay claim to, but it is unique to have a language crafted specifically around this purpose.

And crafted it is—Sanskrit means "synthesized" or "composed." Like classical Arabic and biblical Hebrew, Sanskrit's literary greatness eventually accorded it a mystical prominence—a language of God. Rules of grammar were written as pithy aphorisms and still go by the name of sutras (meaning "threads"), a synonym for scripture. As for its difficulty, take the word "lotus," central in Indian religions. The word in Sanskrit has over fifty variants. Roots, like *biblio* and *oculi*, with which you create new words number over ten thousand in Sanskrit, making the potential vocabulary almost uncountable.

Unsurprisingly, a vast lexicon and difficult grammar do not transfer well, and by the third century BC, local vernaculars had emerged. Known as Prakrits, they whittled down the grammar and carved out their own regional varieties—what eventually evolved into Indo-Aryan languages, such as Gujarati, Bengali, Hindi, Urdu, and so on. By the time of Gautama Buddha, a Prakriti called Pali was used for writing down the Buddha's teachings, while the Buddha himself spoke a Prakrit known as Magadhi.

Sanskrit today is the mother language of very few, if any. Those who choose to learn it are a small, intellectual elite, with an interest in the language's prestige, its linguistic formidability, and its ability to give readers access to its literature. Pretty much the story of Sanskrit's life.

As for its descendants, the most widely spoken are Hindi and Urdu (the Hindi of Pakistan, written in Arabic script and with more Persian/Arabic loanwords), speakers of which can be found all around the world. Many Hindi speakers will salute with the English "cheers," but for special occasions, if you would like to honor or congratulate your friend or co-worker on his success, you can raise a glass of rice wine and say *ek jam __ ke naam,* "to the honor of __."

48

INDONESIAN

"Bersulang"
(ber'soo'lang)

("Toast")

You can lead a Germanic language across the water, but you can't make it stick. No language knows this better than Dutch. Despite a three-hundred-year colonial reign in fifteen countries and thirteen prosperous trading posts, Dutch merchants successfully exported their language exactly three times: Suriname; the islands of the Caribbean Netherlands, and South Africa, where it bred with local dialects and became Afrikaans.

But what happened to the Dutch-speaking Japanese traders in Dejima? Died out. In the Americas? Bullied out by the Portuguese and the British. In Indonesia? What Dutch speakers? During the long and prosperous reign of the fabled Dutch East Indies, the Dutch language was never actually used to conduct business among the natives. There was nothing like the Portuguese Jesuit missionaries to set up schools and teach the locals.

What Dutch merchants had to work with was a smattering of Malay picked up from Malacca. Javanese was considered too difficult to learn, and seeing as how much of Indonesia could already speak some Malay, by the eighteenth century this was made the official language of policy. Together with a long list of Dutch loanwords and the loans of some seven hundred languages native to Indonesia, it was this standardized (and usually poorly spoken) Malay that provided the foundation for Indonesian (the Bahasa that sometimes appears simply means "language").

As a somewhat shoddy construct, the language was overwhelmingly successful—42 million speakers and counting. Most Indonesians have no problem communicating in Indonesian, but they prefer their native languages. Sundanese is a little way from Indonesian with its 27 million speakers, but Javanese has catapulted way beyond—75 million.

You can probably get away with saying *bersulang*, meaning "toast," wherever you go, but on the island of Java, it would be more appropriate to offer *rahayu*, or "peace." Raising and clinking glasses is not unheard of, but it's not exactly popular.

When in Java, tourists are likely to sample some of the world-famous *kopi gayo* (coffee), served either *kopi tubruk* (with sugar and hot water) or *kopi susu* (with sweetened, condensed milk). Despite its popularity, coffee drinking in Bali or Java does not come equipped with the formalized rituals found in Ethiopia. Drinking preferences depend heavily on where you are: a popular rice wine called *brem bali* is drunk on Bali, but on Kalimantan Island (Borneo), *tuak*, or palm liquor, is preferred. There's also Bintang beer—a lager known as Indonesian Heineken.

49

JAPANESE

乾杯
(kan'pie)

("Dry glass")

There are many aspects of Japanese culture Americans have a hard time wrapping their heads around. Kentucky Fried Chicken for Christmas. *Kawaii* and Hello Kitty fandom (and a Hello Kitty–themed bullet train).

207

Three complex writing systems. Add to this that apart from the court of Louis XIV, Japanese culture is home to the most bewildering rules of etiquette in the world. But when it comes to drinking, the idea is astonishingly simple: get hammered.

The idea may be simple, but the reasons for it are a bit more complex. In the tidy Japanese business hierarchy, businessmen with the most years and experience sit comfortably at the top while newcomers struggle well, well below. Strict rules of decorum keep the two classes from ever crossing paths during daylight—or "dry"—business hours, but at night there is the so-called water trade, *mizu shobai*, when seniority and newcomer alike can comingle in karaoke clubs and *izakayas*. In these circumstances, newcomers are expected to become so drunk that they forget all about decorum and actually speak their minds.

Officially, this process requires just one beer, after which, drunk is officially declared, and the free flow of ideas can begin. Although these are technically "wet" office hours, anything foolish said while drunk will be forgotten by the next morning, although the subtext will be remembered. Drunkenness is the grease for the wheel of commerce and as necessary for business as telephones.

Anyone who takes part in a Japanese drinking session will probably notice that most of what is being drunk is beer. This was a change that took place in the 1950s when the Japanese switched over from sake to suds. The reason for this was twofold: beer was modern, hip, and Western—everything Japan wanted to promote about itself. Also, by brewing beer, Japanese industries started a rivalry with American companies,

TASTING NOTE
local beers,
shochu rice
alcohol,
Yamazaki
whiskeys,
umeshu
plum wine.

which, in 1958, produced the extremely popular Asahi steel can of beer. Four other breweries—Kirin, Sapporo, Suntory, and Orion—promptly picked up their rates of beer production, and Japan's renown as a successful brewer was established. Japan also pursued the same tactics with its whiskeys, one of which, Suntory Old, was first exported to the United States in 1961.

But drinking in Japan is very different from drinking in the United States, and toasting requires quite a bit more presentation as well. For one, beer will be served in a small glass, and you will always have either a partner or a group to drink with. As a rule, the host always pours for the guest before pouring for himself. To show politeness, you can try (but not really *try*) to wrest the bottle from him in order to pour his drink, and when he doesn't surrender the bottle, apologize for your failure to fill his. You will then take the glass with your dominant hand and place your other hand underneath, fingers locked and palm flat. As you are a guest and highly honored, your partner will lower his cup below yours. The correct protocol here is to then lower your own. If your partner tries lowering his again, stop him before his glass passes beneath yours and then quickly clink glasses with a *kan pai*. It takes time and practice to master a good kan pai, and after so many drinks, the ritual tends to melt away.

One more thing. As *kan pai* literally means "dry glass," you'll be expected to chug each of your drinks. Failure to do so might earn the chant *ikki ikki*, or "chug." However, simply deferring might signify that you're modest, in which case you'll be encouraged even more to drink up. To unwind yourself from the chug-till-you-drop trap, simply tell your companion firmly that you don't want to drink any further and your wish will be respected. A final note: if you know the Italian cheers *chin-chin* (you do now), absolutely refrain from saying it. The toast comes from a dirty Japanese word for penis.

50

KHMER

"ជល់កែវមួយ"
(chol kaev mouy)

("Let's hit glasses")

Remember the Reliant Regal from
the Mr. Bean skits? That's the
blue, three-wheeled car that
whenever it met with Bean
always ended up on its
side or on its head.

Precisely because they're hardly titans of the road, a nice three-wheeled rickshaw is just about the best thing you can ask for if you're going to be navigating the dusty and ill-paved back roads of Southeast Asia.

In Cambodia, where Khmer is spoken, the name of the ubiquitous rickshaw is *tuk-tuk*. You'll learn it plenty fast. In Siem Reap, you'll find tuk-tuk drivers in all the haunts tourists like to frequent. They're hard-working and generally quite friendly despite the language barrier. Tip your tuk-tuk a couple bucks for shuttling you out to see the sunrise at Angkor Wat, and he might give you a hug. Around afternoon you'll find them napping in hammocks strung between two corners on the inside of their cars, and it's not a bad idea for you to follow their example.

At night, invite your tuk-tuk driver to share a beer, kick back, and *lerk laive lang*— "raise a glass." If you're with a bigger group, offer them a *chol kaev mouy*, meaning something like "let's hit glasses." It won't be the only time you say it. Throughout your beer, you and your group will probably say the words close to a dozen times, and if you do it correctly, the last cheers ought to signify bottoms up.

When lounging with your tuk-tuk driver, have him regale you about the wonders of the ancient Cambodian country. The country really is ancient—archaeological findings report the remains of primitive hunter-gatherers dating to as far back as 5000 BC—and it really is wonderful. Nothing can express this better than the temples and monuments of the Angkor Empire. There, in stupas and *gopuras*, colonettes, statues, pediments and prangs, on bas-reliefs, doors, windows, and walls, and in the slow but inevitable demolition by the gargantuan fig trees with their throttling roots, you can read the whole history and decline of one of the most fascinating kingdoms ever built.

TASTING NOTE
Sombai
liqueurs,
Anchor,
Angkor beers.

The roots themselves and their snakelike embrace even seem to be enacting a kind of creation myth in reverse: according to Cambodian mythology, the country was the dowry to Brahma from the father of a wealthy Naga princess. The Naga in the Indian religions are a deity descended from a king cobra, and among the statues of Angkor Wat (and in other temples), the seven-headed Naga cobra is a common and auspicious figure. His seven heads stand for the seven races of the Naga, each of which is associated with a different color of the rainbow.

Maybe you're not the kind of person who gets excited about colorful snake heads, and that's OK, but you ought to get excited about Sombai. More than just the preeminent liquor of Siem Riep, Sombai is brewed with paired flavors not traditionally associated with spirits. There are eight varieties in total—with flavor combinations such as banana and cinnamon, coconut and pineapple, mango and green chili, and so on— and the liquor also comes packaged in beautiful, hand-painted bottles artfully depicting the temples and traditions of Cambodia.

KOREAN

"건배"
(gone bae)

("Dry glass")

It doesn't take much to do the cha-cha, but what about the cha cha cha cha? What about the cha cha cha cha *cha?* No, Korea doesn't have an unhealthy fixation with Latin dance, but it does have the highest shots-per-week consumption rate in the world, plus one of the most interesting nightlife cultures in Asia.

It all starts with 일차, *il-cha*: round 1. *Cha* (literally "car") is just the term used to designate certain periods in your bar crawl, for bar crawl it must be. Korean culture abhors stationary drinking, and the whole function of the cha is to wheel your drunk butts from bar to bar. Changing chas is a kind of celebration in and of itself, and each cha has a separate name: second cha is *e cha*, third is *sam cha*, fourth is *sah cha*, then *oh cha*, then drunk. Getting drunk involves its whole subculture heavily lubricated with soju, a spirit of about 17 percent alcohol, drunk neat.

For one thing, you will always be in a group and many times on business. As in Japan, Korean honorifics, or honorary forms of address, play a huge role in how you address your superiors or inferiors, affecting not just how you call the person but what verb you use and how that person answers your questions. Imagine being a secretary at a prominent bank—we'll call you Min-jun—and going out for drinks with not only fellow employees but also your bosses and your CEO. You go to pour a drink for your table, see a bottle of soju sitting next to your CEO—we'll call him Mr. Kim—and ask him to pass the bottle. Now, most of us would probably ask for the bottle superpolitely: "Excuse me, Mr. Kim, if it isn't too much trouble would you mind" and so on, but not in Korea. Instead you might say it more like, "Hey, Kim! Gimme that bottle!" and Mr. Kim, amazingly enough, probably would, with an "Of course, Mr. Min-jun."

This awkward phenomenon is known as *yaja* time. It's just plain weird. The idea is that once the group decides to play yaja time, all honorifics are reversed, and you talk down to superiors while they talk up to you. Naturally you'll want to test the playing field and make sure your superiors are cool with being messed with before fully committing yourself, but if they agree, anything goes. Anything includes giving them punishment shots (*buljoo*) for breaking the rules of any other games you have going on. In addition to drinking shots, you'll also be putting away *poktanju* (bomb drink), Korea's boilermaker, usually a shot of soju or whiskey in a beer.

As far as how to drink, raise your glass with both hands with the rest of the group, call *gonebae*, and then block the side of the mouth that faces your superior. If he's sitting on your right side, use your left hand to drink and your right hand to block, and vice versa. If you're in the middle, use both hands while taking your shot. And if you don't drink or can't drink anymore and have just been given a buljoo? In this case, you've got a safe route, albeit a perilous one. For girls this is called a *heuk-gi-sa* (black knight), and for boys, a *heuk-iang-mi* (black rose). A "rose" or a "knight" is someone who will finish your shot for you in exchange for one wish. The upside to this is you get a get-out-of-shot-free card. And the downside? If your black knight or rose refuses you, you'll be given another buljoo as punishment on top of your punishment.

52

MALAYALAM

"ചിയഴ്സ്"
(cheers)

("Cheers")

Ever wondered what the Florida Everglades would look like if you replaced all the alligators with elephants? Welcome to Kerala, the southwestern cultural hotbed and one of the most elephant-populated states in India, with a plethora of elephant sanctuaries to boot.

221

TASTING NOTE
sambharam
buttermilk
beverage,
kallu palm
toddy.

According to the Hindu myth, the warrior Parasur-ama was made to do penance for killing all of the males of the ruling caste, the Kshatriyas. Approaching the northern sea, he tossed his axe (*parasu*) into the waters, and the spot where the waters gave up the land is called Kerala. Depending on which side you listen to, the name Kerala is a synthesis of Malayalam words meaning "land of coconuts" or an ancient form of Tamil that means "land of the *cheras*" (a chera being a lake) or possibly "sandy place."

Kerala supplies 45 percent of India's coconuts, and its backwaters are known the world around. One of the most touristcentric destinations in India, Kerala began marketing itself as "God's Own Country" back in the 1980s, and their campaign has drawn rapidly increasing numbers of guests ever since. The region was even named by *National Geographic* as one of the top 50 destinations of a lifetime, and if paradise evokes images of breaking waves on honey-coloreds shores, you don't get closer than this. So pristine are the beaches that Ayurvedic-themed resorts are on the rise with treatments servicing every kind of detox imaginable: emotional, bodily, spiritual, social, intellectual. Or maybe all you want is to make pottery and drink wine, in which case there's a resort for that as well. Or maybe you'd rather skim around some backwater estuaries in a luxury houseboat? There are services for that, and for anything you might wish to do once aboard, including fishing for carp and snakehead fish, taking out canoes, or getting your fix on in a local toddy shop.

Unsurprising for the land of coconuts, natives use fermented water from their native fruit to brew a toddy called *kallu*, which can either be weak cider or spirit-level strong depending on how early or late you happen on by. These shacks are filled with easygoing locals whom you can salute with Malayalam "cheers," pronounced the same as in English.

Outside of the backwaters, however, you might have some difficulty finding a good watering hole. Government crackdowns due to the high rates of alcoholism have prohibited the sale of hard alcohol

to all but special state-owned shops and some luxury hotels, meaning bars and restaurants sell nothing but beer and wine. While strict on its alcohol, Kerala is famously loose when it comes to beef, being one of the only states in India where you can eat and purchase real beef products, otherwise illegal in Hindu-dominated India.

53

MALAY

"Yum seng"
(yahm sen)

("Dry glass")

Trade plays a wild card when it comes to moving languages around. The effects can be either tremendous for the language (as with English), or else the language becomes swamped by the vast amount of other tongues it mingles with, like what happened to the Phoenician of the trad-ers in ancient Canaan.

A stranger fate occurs when a language of trade patronizes one other than its own—the situation of the Dutch East India company in Malaysia and Indonesia, whose vehicle of transaction was Malay.

This was a practical decision. It was much easier for merchants to pick up a bit of Malay than for them to teach Dutch to a large foreign population. Even after approximately two centuries of trade, in today's Malaysia you find virtually zero Dutch influence in the roughly 130 languages. A typical Malaysian has compulsory education in Malay and English at school, while at home Malay Muslims take on Arabic; Indians, Tamil; and Chinese, Mandarin in addition to another dialect, such as Cantonese, Hokkien, or Hakka. And then there are the indigenous tongues: Iban, Bidayuh, or Dusun by the tribes in Sabah and Sarawak, in the state of Borneo.

Cantonese Chinese, imported from the south of China, is what gives Malay it's most popular toast—*yum sing*—but regional languages have plenty to add. Make it over to Borneo, the Malaysian state that shares the island with Indonesia, and you may find yourself in Sarawak, dominated by the Iban tribe. The Iban people dwell in enormous communal cabins, longhouses, where up to eighty families can be housed. The people are famous as both gracious hosts and as headhunters. The latter is no longer practiced, thankfully, though severed human skulls of vanquished enemies still decorate some of the rooms of the longhouse and are available for viewing, so long as you can pass through the crucible of an Iban greeting. What will happen is that your host will appear at the threshold with a shot glass of rice wine—*tuak*—take the first sip, and then pass the shot to you. Drain it off, and you may enter. The communal shot glass is an essential part of the culture and unfortunately can't be dismissed for reasons of hygiene, no matter how many people end up sharing it in a single drinking session.

The Iban have no word for "cheers"—instead, you throw your head back and shout, "Oahhhaa!" for as long as you want. If you want to instigate the drinking session, you can hustle your friends out the door by saying *aram ngirup* (let's go drink), or in Malay, *jom minum*. But this is just the Iban.

In Sarawak, there are the Bidayuh—a term for the collected tribes of the Land Dayak groups, and they have a similar communal aspect to their culture. For toasting, there is this rapid tongue patter, "Tara tara tara oohhh!" In Sabah, also in Borneo, you'll say *aramaiti*, meaning "come together."

TASTING NOTE
Chamisul and Chum Churum soju, *makgeolli* rice wine, local teas.

227

54

NEPALI

"चयिर्स"
(cheers)

("Cheers")

We use it or a variation in virtually every conversation, but does anyone ever stop and think about what's behind the word "hello"? Only about 140 years, as things would turn out. Before then, it was "hullo."

TASTING NOTE
jaand rice beer,
Everest and
Nepali Ice beer,
chyyang
traditional
rice wine,
homemade
raksi, *aila*
liquor, lassi
yoghurt
beverage.

The word went through several permutations—"hal-loo," "helli," "hillo"—and was originally used to summon one's hunting dogs. Today, the *Cambridge English Dictionary* defines it as simply an "exclamation," and why should a greeting mean anything else? Fair point, but it simply isn't the case everywhere else.

Nepalis don't say "hullo" or "hello" but rather *namaste* and *namaskar*, the former of which is taken from the Sanskrit roots *namah* (perform obeisance) and *te* (to you): "I bow to you." Actually, Nepalis say quite a bit more than just this.

This relatively small country can get a little crazy when it comes to languages—123 languages all told, a side effect of mountains. If you go north, you'll probably encounter the Sherpa people, who will greet you with *tashi delek*, taken from neighboring Tibet (and meaning something like "may everything be well"). Over at Kathmandu Valley, you may encounter some Newars; your word here is *jwajwalapa (jwo ja lo pa)*, and your toast will be *chhaang*, also the name of a millet beer. And on the border with China just north of Kathmandu, you can find Tamang speakers who will hail you with *lasso*.

After the greeting comes a good show of generosity, something the people of Nepal has down pat. Strangers will invite you into their homes, serve you *dhal bhat* (cooked lentils with rice), make rapid chitchat whether you understand it or not, and ply you with enough homemade *raksi* to make your head swim. Raksi is alcohol made from millet or rice, usually at home distilleries. Its function is recreational as well as religious: it is used as an offering to Vedic gods and goddesses in festivals and in purification rituals following the death of a family member. There's plenty of casual drinking too but it's generally in the countryside and among ethnic groups, such as the Sherpa or Newari. If you find yourself in the company of some rural locals and a bottle of raksi, do not try matching your companions drink for drink. You will lose, and you will lose hard. All this said, Nepalis in the cities adhere to a stricter near-abstinence and generally don't imbibe except during special occasions. As for "cheers," Nepali simply defers to the English.

55

SINHALA

"ජය වේවා"
(jaya viva)
("Cheers")

Ceylon country is tea country until the coconuts get involved. Sri Lankan palms are regularly tapped to brew a very special alcohol called *arrack*, generally bottled and labeled VSOA, "Very Special Old Arrack."

TASTING NOTE
Ceylon tea,
kithul ra
palm wine,
Elephant House
ginger beer,
Lion Lager.

Arrack in this sense does not mean the same as the Batavian arrack of Indonesia; nor is it the arrack/raki liquors of the Mediterranean or the wine of the Philippines. *Arak* comes from an Arabic term for "juice" or "sweet," which was shuffled by Arabic traders across so many seaboards it became a default term for alcohol.

The arrack of Sri Lanka refers to a rum-like liquor aged in oak barrels and distilled from the nectar of coconut blossoms. This is collected by tree-climbing "toddy tappers," although because coconut sap will begin fermenting as soon as it is collected, some villages in rural communities forego having their nectar aged and simply drink it off straight, as a liquor called *kithul ra* (*kithul* is Sinhala for "fishtail palm"). If you find yourself in rural Sri Lanka, you can probably sample some, although I imagine the arrack might go down better.

Sri Lankans speak Sinhala, an Indo-Aryan language that climbed down from the north of India and then evidently leapfrogged across the Dravidian-speaking regions of the south and landed smack on the island, which, at the time (around 200 BC), may have been (but probably wasn't) infested with lions. That is to say, the real live bone-crunching, human-devouring kind. Other kinds of lions are still in abundance. One holds a sword on the Sri Lankan flag. You can see the stone paws of another creep out from the awe-inspiring Sigiriya fortress. The highest-selling beer in the country is—you guessed it—a lager called Lion. And the word *Sinhala* comes from the Sanskrit for "lion." Serendipitous? The word wouldn't be out of place.

Actually for a while, the word *was* the place, at least to the Romans, Arabs, and Persians for whom Sri Lanka was known as Serendivis, Serandib, and Serendip respectively, a corruption of the Sanskrit name Sinhaladvipa, meaning "the island where lions dwell." During the time of the Roman astronomer Ptolemy, Sri Lanka was known as Salike, and later Sailan/Silan, which eventually became the name Ceylon—the word used for the British colony until 1972. *Lanka* was there for some time too—the word appears in the Indian epic Ramayana and means "glittering"—but it didn't get the Sanskrit honorific *sri* (meaning "beautiful") until the 1950s. That's quite a long time to have to wait for the right name to come.

"Tagay"
(ta'gay)

("Chug")

Why are Austronesian languages so much fun? For one, they can be quite a bit easier than many other languages on the market. Malay and Indonesian make plurals by simply repeating the nouns:
one book is *buku*
and books,
buku-buku.

56

TAGALOG

Samoan and Tahitian all share similar words, such as "canoe," *va'a*, and Hawaiian frequently does away with verbs like "be" and "have," rendering the statement "I am a fisherman," into "Fisherman I."

But the best part has got to be the tongue twisters, of which Tagalog is king. This redundant sentence: "A Kabkab frog, croaking, it was just croaking, now it's croaking again," is deliciously rendered in Tagalog as "Palakang Kabkab, kumakalabukab, kaka-kalabukab pa lamang, kumakalabukab na naman." And my favorite "Will we go down? Yes, we will go down" becomes "Bababa ba? Bababa!" The language sounds like it's already had a few, and chances are you will too when you're vacationing in the Philippines.

Filipinos are as inclusive as inclusive gets when it comes to drinking culture, and the tradition can be both a blessing and a curse. To begin with, *tagays* (shots) are always exchanged in small groups of people, usually sitting in a circle (and many times right on the side of the street). This group element is crucial. It references early years of Filipino history and communal rationing, practices that had been in effect possibly as early as the time of Ferdinand Magellan's arrival in 1521, and certainly by 1630 when the word *tagay* and its modern meaning appears in the *Miguel Ruiz Spanish Vocabulariou*, alongside an impressive drinking lexicon: 1. *managay*, meaning to deal out shots; 2. *tagayan*, person dealing shots; 3. *papanagayin*, the person taking the shot; 4. *ipapanàgay*, a kind of wine; and 5. *catagayan*, a drinking vessel.

Unbelievably, many of these words persist. There are still tagayans, only they refer to the glasses used to fill the other glasses, and the *tanggero* is the person in charge of dealing the drinks. The pouring goes around in a circle, everyone chants *tagay*, and the drinks go down. You may need to rouse your tanggero if he or she's not vigilant: this is done with the short rhyme: "Tagay pa, alak pa!" ("More shots, more liquor!")

Now, here's the kicker. For any invitation to tagay that is extended to you, even from a stranger (especially from a stranger!), the proper and polite protocol is to sit down and accept, wherever it may be taking place. Depending on where you are, you will either be given your own shot glass or expected to share the same one with the rest of the group. Comradery trumps hygiene.

You'll most likely be taking shots of beer—San Miguel or the ever popular Red Horse—but you might also get a healthy dose of the national liquor, *lambanóg*, or coconut arrack. Coconut is something of an over-simplification: you can buy cinnamon-, blueberry-, mango-, and even bubblegum-flavored lambanóg. One shot should be good enough to secure the respect of your friends; however, if you choose to stay longer, it might do to take your tagay with a more elaborate toast, such as *para sa tagumpay* (for success). Also, if your drinking group is superstitious, the first shot might be "for the devil," in which case it is to be thrown into the corner.

57

TAMIL

"மகிழ்ச்சி"
(magil'chi)

("Happiness")

When it comes to languages in India, there's a neat divide between the two prominent families, like the Corleones and the Tattaglias in *The Godfather*.

241

TASTING NOTE
sambaram
buttermilk
beverage,
wine palm
(alcohol is
banned in
Tamil Nadu).

About 75 percent of Indians speak an Indo-Aryan language such as Hindi, Gujarati, Pubjabi, or Bengali, and 15–19 percent a Dravidian, which is where Tamil and its close relative Malayalam fall (along with two other siblings, Telugu and Kannada). Indo-Aryans are generally spoken from as far north as Pakistan and Nepal down to the center of India, and the southern areas are dominated by the Dravidians. The pattern has plenty of irregularities—Dravidian languages show up in the southern parts of Pakistan, Afghanistan, Nepal, Bhutan, and some Southeast Asian countries while the Indo-Aryan language Sinhalese dominates Sri Lanka—but generally it's consistent.

Indian languages also employ a wide variety of scripts, all of them descendants from the Brahmi script first used in India in the first millennium BC. Although the method is far from perfect, you can make a guess at what family the language belongs to by taking a look at its script. Most Indo-Aryans use the Devanagari alphabet or a permutation of it, which is notable for the horizontal line that links the tops of the letters. Dravidian scripts are often loopier and jumpier. Here are three kinds of Devanagari versus three kinds of loopier Brahmi script, the word spelling out the language: नेपाली (Nepali), বাঙালি (Bengali) ਪੰਜਾਬੀ (Punjabi) and then தமிழ் (Tamil), മലയാളം (Malayalam), ಕನ್ನಡ (Kannada). Variations on the jumpy Brahmi can also be found throughout Southeast

Asia, thanks to ancient Buddhist missionaries. Thus, you get ไทย in Thailand, ລາວ in Laos, and မြန်မာ in Myanmar.

So what else is different about these two families? Sanskrit is said to share a common ancestor with Iranian Old Avestan, the language used to compose the Zoroastrian scriptures of the sixth century BC. The first Sanskrit inscriptions are said to date between the first and third centuries BC, roughly equivalent to when Tamil inscriptions made their appearance in Tamil Nadu and Sri Lanka, between the first and second centuries BC, but these dates are difficult to appraise. There's an ongoing debate about whether Tamil predates Sanskrit or the other way around, which is too messy to go into here. Historically, Tamil culture has been superseded by its prestigious neighbor, so it's easy to see why the language wants the prestige. Many people know something about the Sanskrit philosophical epics, but who's heard of the Silappatikaram?

In contrast to Kannada and Malayalam, Tamil *does* contain an original word for cheers: *magil'chi*, meaning "happiness." Though wine, beer, and spirits are now drunk throughout Tamil-speaking states and countries (including Sri Lanka and Malaysia), older Tamil culture had families brewing a special fruit punch called *nungu* from the trunk of the *Borassus flabellifer*, variously nicknamed the doub palm, toddy palm, or wine palm.

58

THAI

"ไชโย"
(chai'yo)

("Cheers")

There are plenty of reasons why Thailand deserves its nickname "Land of a Thousand Smiles."

24

TASTING NOTE
Chang and
Singha beers,
Mekhong and
SangSom
rums.

Guests are invariably happy with the country's beautiful beaches, cheap alcohol, eternal sunshine, and pleasant temperatures (an average low of 71 degrees in December). Plus, the Thai people are some of the friendliest, most accepting, and easygoing people the world has got.

During a recent trip, a stranger stopped my two friends and me at a park in Bangkok to wish us a happy Makha Bucha Day: a holiday commemorating the day the Buddha revealed some of his most important philosophies to a spontaneous crowd of followers. He then proceeded to map out for us all the city's best temples, hailed us a tuk-tuk, and wished us all the blessings of the Buddha.

Unfortunately, Thailand is better known for its seedier sex side—a place of snickers rather than smiles. Sex, smiles, snickers: you can find whatever you want and don't want down a ten-minute stroll of Bangkok's infamous Khaosan Road. The street is lined with hostels, bars, dance clubs, and vendors hawking everything from dirty bracelets and fake IDs to fried grasshoppers. The ones who stick it out for long here after dark are generally the young, adventurous and/or drunk types, and if you're any combination of the three, your cab driver will probably try steering you in the direction of a local Ping-Pong show. Fair warning: these are always bad ideas. Although they don't necessarily equate to live sex, Ping-Pong shows generally have a measure of it alongside a variety of acts demonstrating, for example, alternative methods of smoking cigarettes and different ways of bouncing Ping-Pong balls into cups. I'd advise you not to go, but depending on how many you've had or on what you've had, you might make the decision to take your cabbie up on his offer regardless. In that case, find a place to sit in the far back and one hundred percent avoid volunteering for anything the performers ask you to do.

If you're in Bangkok more than one night and want an alternative risqué experience, there are plenty of ladyboy performances for an experience unlike any other. Ladyboy cabarets are celebrations of all things glitzy, glamorous, and gay, with generally high production values and good performances from some of the most beautiful transgender women on the planet, including ladyboy Liza Minnellis, ladyboy Rihannas, and ladyboy Celine Dions. If you're a straight guy showing up at one of these, bring a good sense of humor and a Thai level of easygoingness: the first ten minutes are going to be pretty awkward.

Thais raise rather than clink their glasses when saying *chai'yo*. You can also use *chokh di*—it means "good luck."

59

VIETNAMESE

"Chúc sức khoẻ"
(chook soo kway)

("Good health")

If you order a beer in the summertime in a respectable restaurant in the United States, tap, can, or bottle, you can probably expect it to come in or with a chilled glass.

249

This is one of those small but remarkable amenities you get to appreciate more and more the longer you spend boozing in a foreign country. Meanwhile, the rest of the world knocks back their brews at room temperature and doesn't really mind what it's missing.

If you want your beer served cold but you want to avoid stares, after the United States you'll need to go as far as Vietnam, where the beer is cheap, abundant, and comes served up with ice cubes. Ice cubes in beer? This is one of those dumb prejudices you never realized you had until you were served a glass of Bia Hanoi with three dainty cubes bobbing at the surface. Won't that water the beer down? It sure will, but since beer is already 95 percent water, who really gives a damn? Especially if you're in a steamy Saigon bar and the temperature is 105, and you can cool down either by drinking a beer or jumping in a lake. In the hot months (which are all the months), iced beer is just something you learn to expect with your day, like coffee, which, in Vietnam, comes in small cups loaded with condensed milk and sugar.

A typical beer generally runs around twenty-five cents, making beer the de facto beverage for any large drinking group. And drinking group it will probably be if you are staying in either of the country's major cities, Hanoi or Ho Chih Minh. The Vietnamese are welcoming and friendly, and it's not unknown for a stranger to approach your table (if you're a group) to offer a toast.

As many Vietnamese speak excellent English, you can count on hearing a good number of "cheers," but this is not at all the way to toast if you're prepping up for a wild night. Boozers will get on their feet and bellow, "Một hai ba dzô!" (*mote hi ba yo*, "One, two, three, cheers!"). This is followed by a smashing of glasses, and then it's bottoms up—*cạn ly* (*gan lee*), unless you're not feeling up to the challenge, at which point you may be chided for failing to give *một trăm phần tram* (*mot jam ben jam*, "give 100 percent"). But this is a drink-to-get-drunk rule, and if you've got an early morning or just don't feel like a crazy night and want to decline respectfully, you can reply that you're only going to go *năm mươi phần tram* (*nam muy ben jam*, 50 percent). Finally, if you're sharing a quiet respectful drink and not a drink-to-get-drunk drink, you can clink glasses with the words *chúc sức khoẻ* (*chook soo way*), meaning simply "good health."

251

PART FOUR

AFRICA AND THE MIDDLE EAST

60

AFRIKAANS

"Gesondheid"
(he'zond'heit)

("Good health")

What separates a language from a dialect? A trading army. Welcome to Afrikaans—the Dutch language's most successful export! Hence why Afrikaans *gesondheid* (health) looks suspiciously like Dutch *gezondheid*. How did Dutch even wind up in South Africa in the first place? Let's go back to the year 1652.

Merchants of the Dutch East India Company have arrived and set up a resupply station off the Cape of Good Hope—from here, it's a straight shot to the Indian subcontinent, then Malacca. Now, South Africa may not sound like it's very close to India or Malaysia, but if you're a seventeenth-century merchant, east is much more of a destination rather than a geographical position. For sailors, the cape marked the first point in the journey when you could finally stop going south. The settlement at the cape (Cape Town) eventually became lucrative enough for the British Empire to do to the Dutch what the Dutch had successfully done to the Portuguese in Malaysia and Indonesia. With the Anglo-Saxon treaty in 1814, Dutch colonial rule in South Africa came to an official halt, close to 150 years since the year it started.

The ironic thing is that South Africa wouldn't have ever figured into Dutch trading plans if the Indies trading vessel—the *Nieuwe Haarlem*—hadn't shipwrecked off the cape in 1647. A few years later, a merchant named Jan Van Riebeek convinced the company to reopen the settlement the refugees had abandoned, and thus—from a shipwreck, then an opportunity—a colonial power was born.

So what does that make Afrikaans? Depending on who you ask, it can be all kinds of things. Three hundred years ago it was referred to as "Cape Dutch," and today some Dutch and Afrikaans speakers call it "Baby Dutch." It is the language of *aardvark*, *meerkat*, *springbok*, and *trek*. Arguments rage trying to determine its status between creole (developed from a mix of other languages), partial creole, or Dutch daughter. Afrikaans speakers abroad are fiercely proud of it and are happy to show off its snarls and its glottal scrapes, like it was a pet Rottweiler.

You'll get an excellent sampling of this mighty tongue, with this popular boozing rhyme, if you're out on the town with any Afrikaans-speaking comrades. (Warning: explicit content follows.) "Ek sien hom, hy blink nie. Ek ruik hom, hy stink nie. Ek hoor hom, hy klink nie. So wie de' fok sê ek mag hom nie drink nie! Mag hy val waar hy will, net nie op die fokken grond nie!" (I see him, but he doesn't shine. I smell him, but he doesn't stink. I hear him, but he doesn't make a sound. So who the fuck says I'm not allowed to drink him! Let him fall where he wants, just not on the fucking ground!)

TASTING NOTE
Castle lager
and local beers,
*mampoer/
witblits*
moonshine,
Van der Hum
liqueur, Amarula
Cream liqueur,
local wines.

257

61

AMHARIC

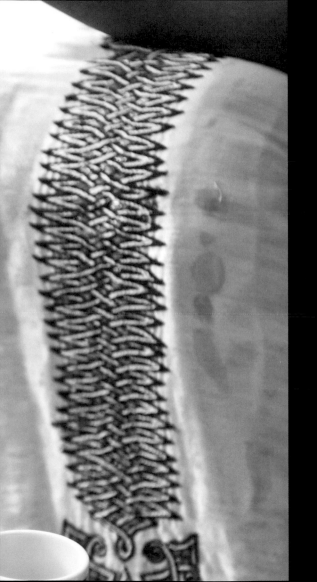

"ለጤናችን"
(letenachin)

("To health")

Welcome to coffee country. Ethiopia's number one product—coffee revenue is responsible for as much as 60 percent of the economy. The arabica coffee bean is believed to have originated in Ethiopia as far back as the ninth century.

The legend goes that a shepherd first discovered the famous coffee plant over a thousand years ago when his caffeinated goats, having nibbled some of the berries, got up on their hind legs and began to dance. Take the story however you want, but nothing expresses the Ethiopian reliance on coffee better than the proverb "Buna dabo Naw" (Coffee is our bread).

Ethiopians pay homage to the crop through an elaborate ritual, which also functions as a social powwow. Generally, coffee takes place once a day (sometimes more often) and is composed of three separate parts: *abol*, *tona*, and *baraka*. Those who are lucky enough to be invited to take part in the drinking ceremony are expected to drink at least three cups, not only for social politeness (and to make sure you're *really* awake) but for the blessing that the baraka (third drink) is considered to bestow on the soul of the drinker. If you are a guest in an Ethiopian household, you can expect to be served a cup of coffee once you cross the threshold into the house—it ought to be noted too that coffee ceremonies can take as long as an hour, so just cool your jets and settle in. And when you receive your coffee, make sure you pronounce the honorary coffee toast: *q'onjo bunna* (good coffee).

Also known as Abyssinian, Amharic has been around since the end of the fourteenth century. It's the second largest Semitic language in the world (after Arabic but in front of Hebrew) and lays claim to two unique religions—Ethiopian Orthodoxy and Rastafari (from *rast* "chief" and *tafari*, "feared"), whose most famous member is certainly Bob Marley.

During his travels there, Marley even took the Ethiopian name Berhane Selassie—Selassie after Haile Selassie, the former emperor of Ethiopia and also incarnation of God according to many Rastafarians.

As for alcohol, Ethiopians drink a fizzy, gold-colored concoction known as *tej* (in Oromo, *daadhi*), which is mead fermented with the African shrub *gesho*. Spirits include the colorless *areki* and the most popular, *tella*, which can be brewed with many different kinds of cereals: barley, wheat, maize, millet, sorghum, and teff. The most commonly drunk alcohol in Ethiopia, tella is called "traditional beer" but is quite sour and much different from Western beer. Some drinkers even put in ash to mitigate the sourness. Before drinking, be sure you say the standard toast *letenachin* (to health) or *lebeteseb* (to family), or you can simply use the English "cheers."

بصحتك
(bese'haltuk)

("In your health")

Arabic Admiral Albatross sits on a satin sofa, snacking on apricots and caraway. He likes lemons and limes, sugar syrup, and jars of soda, puffs a hookah, drinks coffee but not alcohol. I wrote this stupid little ditty not because I had any desire to entertain but rather to give a short demonstration of just how much we owe to Arabic, the language responsible for every one of the nouns in those first two sentences.

62

ARABIC

Whether you're talking textiles, geography, cuisine, or science and math (*algebra*, *algorithm*, *average*, *cube*, and *degree*), Arabic borrowings may sometimes be subtle, but they are many. This isn't a phenomenon found just in English, by the way. Islam-dominated countries obviously pump in boatloads of Arabic (in Central and Southeast Asia as well as in Northern Africa and the Middle East), but you can find Arabic contributions to the vocabulary of languages as close as the Romance languages and as far as Indonesia. There's even a whole Arabic skeletal and muscle system buried beneath the Italian skin of Maltese (whose predominantly Roman Catholic majority refers to God as Allah, to the confusion of everybody).

Arabic's impressive mark on the world is only amplified by the century-long blitzkrieg through which it was dispersed. Before the beginnings of the Islamic conquest in 622, Arabic was a series of dialects spoken among wandering tribes on the Arabian Peninsula, tentatively strung together by a shared literary language. By the year 751, Islam had spread as far east as modern-day Uzbekistan, as far west as Tangier, and had completely overrun both the Iberian and the Arabian Peninsulas. Rarely has a language

had such total success in so short a time (minus, well, English), and rarely has its dominance over other languages been so complete. Formerly powerful tongues such as Egyptian (Coptic) and Greek in Egypt, Berber languages in Libya, Punic/Carthiginian in Tunisia, and Aramaic throughout the Fertile Crescent were all pushed to the outskirts or else forced to take refuge in Christian churches, which to this day is responsible for the continued survival of Coptic and Aramaic.

266

Arabic couldn't help but be influenced by the countries it dominated, and this is exhibited by the large number of dialects. They come in six groups: the Maghrebi (near Morocco, with Berber, or more properly Tamazight, influences), Sudanese (Nubian), Egyptian (Coptic), Arabian Peninsula (the closest to classical Arabic, used in the seventh to ninth centuries), Mesopotamian (Aramaic and Turkish), and Levantine (Aramaic and Canaanite).

As most people know and as the first two sentences clarify, in accord with the Islamic faith, most Arabic speakers are teetotalers. The most famous Arabic toast is the grace *bismallah*, spoken before any kind of eating, drinking, or partaking in any formal/semiformal ceremony. It's also the word everyone mispronounces during the second part of "Bohemian Rhapsody."

All that said, alcohol drinking is not unheard of in the Arabic-speaking belt, and the word *besehaltuk* (in your health) is used specifically for alcohol. Egypt has numerous wineries, such as Gianaclis, Omar Khayyam, Obelisk, and Sahara, which produce both reds and whites. In Lebanon, although wine making has been going on for roughly five thousand years, modern viticulture has only really flourished in the last fifty years or so due to the high-quality vines of the Bekaa Valley. Egyptian and Lebanese Arabic toast with a clink and the expression *fee saḥitkum* (to your health), or *fee sehetyek* when addressing a woman. In Morocco, the expression *besaha* (compare Maltese *sahha*) is used in a similar vein as *bon appetit*.

63

HAUSA

"Don faranta zuciya"
(don faranta zu'siyah)

("Rejoice in your heart")

Finding a European language in East Asia or Africa is a little like finding your cat stuck in your guitar: you're interested to see how it got there, but you're not all that surprised that it's there. With a language from just about any other phylum stuck in a strange place—the Welsh conclave in Argentina, for example—you're likely to get some raised eyebrows.

269

And if you drive a language with some Semitic ancestry (including Hebrew, Arabic, and Aramaic) from as far east as Iraq and drop it off in the heart of western Africa, you've got some explaining to do. Lucky for us, the Hausa have a story that does just this.

The legend goes that after being exiled from his hometown of Baghdad, Prince Bayajidda, along with his wife and a band of warriors, crossed the Sahara and eventually came to rest in the town of Daura, where the prince asked an old woman for a drink of water. The old woman told the prince that a serpent named Sarki was guarding the well, and the people were allowed only one day a week to draw water. Bayajidda confronted the serpent, beheaded it, stuck the head in a bag, and presented it to the queen Magajiya Daurama. For his deed, Bayajidda requested the queen's hand in marriage, but she turned him down and offered him her concubine, Bagwariya, instead. With Bagwariya and eventually with the queen, Bayajidda is said to have fathered the eventual rulers of the seven Hausa states.

You don't go far in Hausa history without bumping into this legend, considered by many to be the essential Hausa foundation myth. Daura (in northern Nigeria) is still considered the spiritual home of the Hausa, and the well, as well as the sword used to slay the serpent, continues to be venerated. At its most basic, the story represents the coming together of two powerful migratory peoples.

Coming together has been the story of the Hausa for centuries, or ever since the prophetic arrival of the Baghdad prince. The Hausa have mixed with dozens of ethnic groups all throughout western and central

Africa, freely with the Fulani in Nigeria (Hausa is sometimes referred to as Hausa-Fulani) although not with the Yoruba and Igbo. There's also quite a bit of runoff from northern Berber tribes—specifically the Tuareg—with Berber-language loanwords flooding Hausa's vocabulary with borrowed terms for sword, turban, and that all-important desert vehicle, the camel.

The Hausa are predominantly Muslim and therefore reluctant to confess to any tippling, but in these fruit-rich countries, juices and smoothies are plentiful. The African cherry, or *agbalumo* fruit, in addition to boasting some impressive health benefits, makes for a tremendous smoothie if paired with sugar cane, simple syrup, saffron, passion fruit, ginger, or whatever else satisfies your palate. If you can get your hands on some palm wine, you've got all the makings of a pretty good cocktail.

Clinks aren't really a part of the culture, but you may hear a kind of toast among the Hausa for special occasions: the beautiful phrase *don faranta zuciya*—"rejoice in your heart."

TASTING NOTE
kunu tiger nut juice, agbalumo cocktail, palm wine.

64

IGBO

"Ekele dịrị"
(ekelee diri)

("Thanksgiving")

Does the power of language mean only that we respect what words have the ability to convey, or does this power go deeper? Can a word well and truly change a person? The Igbo people of southeast Nigeria have a belief in words the Westerners can best describe as mystical.

273

In his 1999 speech "Tomorrow Is Uncertain, Today Is Soon Enough," the great Igbo/Ibo writer Chinua Achebe quotes the proverb "The name given to a man is what he becomes." We're all familiar with Juliet's digression of what's in a name, but would a rose really incite the same sensations if you called it a "burfalump"? How much does a name affect how we see the world or how it sees us?

In Igbo culture, a name represents a meaningful narrative of the life, heritage, hopes, and even despairs of the family. Names can transmit wishes, desires, prayers, and even curses. A child's name can even convey the day on which it was born. The male names Okere, Okafor, Okonkwo, and Okeke and female names Mgbere, Mgbafor, Mgbakwo, and Mgbeke correspond to the four days of the Igbo week. Names like Ihentuge and Nwaruoulo, meaning "What I have been searching for" and "May a child at last reach this house," show the anticipation and long wait of an expectant mother, while a name like Ahamefula—"May my name not be lost"—shows an unabashed desire for family glory. Igbo names also reflect the divide between life (*ndu*) and death (*onwu*). Life is sanctified and celebrated in names like Ndukaku (life is higher than riches), Nduwuisi (life is supreme), and Chijindu (it is God who sustains life). Death is frequently seen as a taskmaster Igbo mothers can petition, negotiate with, or even flatter to spare the newborn: Ikewrionwu (no strength can overcome death), Onwuzuruigb (death reaches all over Igboland), and Onwucheckwa (death, wait a little).

With all this emphasis on short, pithy language, it comes as no surprise that Igbo people greatly value the proverb, what Achebe famously called "the palm oil with which words are eaten." He might also have mentioned that like oil, once you've gotten some proverbs on your hands, it can be very difficult rubbing them off. There are hundreds of these proverbs, but as I am no expert on Igbo culture, I will leave the quoting to someone better versed than me. After all, one who does not drink palm wine should not tap it. In other words, "leave it to the experts."

It's true of proverbs as well as palm wine, which is one of the primary alcohols in Nigeria and drunk both recreationally and for celebrations. A toast among the Igbo is the equivalent of a blessing, and in saying *ekele dịrị*, you are literally saying "thanksgiving." Traditionally, everyone will raise glasses while the person gives the toast, but there is also a tradition in which the toaster produces a hot drink and pours it bit by bit onto the ground as he or she pronounces the components of the blessing, such as happiness (*onu*), success (*oganihu*), peace (*odinamma*), or love (*ihunaya*).

TASTING NOTE
palm wine,
Chapman
cocktail,
ogogoro palm
moonshine.

65

KINYARWANDA

"Ubuzima bwachu"
(ooboo'zima bwa'choo)

("Health")

In Kenya, you get drunk with the *dawa*. In Nigeria, you have palm wine. South Africa has *umqombothi*. And Rwanda? Bananas. In addition to being one of the fastest-growing countries in Africa, Rwanda boasts one of the most innovative ways to get plastered.

277

TASTING NOTE
banana wine,
inkangaza
sorghum beer,
urwagwa
banana beer,
milk.

Banana wine is a thick, lumpy alcohol (rather more like fermented fruit juice) distilled either at home or in larger breweries, the most successful of which is Coproviba, whose ambitions include marketing banana wine for Americans as well as Rwandans. Banana wine isn't fit for all occasions, and many Rwandans keep a bottle in reserve only for greeting guests or for celebrating festivals.

If not banana wine, there's banana beer, *urwagwa*, which is brewed with pulped bananas mixed with sorghum or maize as a source of yeast. Bypassing bananas altogether, you can also find sorghum beer, *ikigage*, or a special type of sorghum beer infused with honey, *inkangaza*, which is drunk on certain festivals. Rwandans will always be eager to toast your health (*ubuzima bwachu*) whether with a glass of ikigage, Primus and Mützig beer, or banana wine, and for nonalcoholic drinks there's *fanta*, an umbrella term for any carbonated drink, and *ikivuguto*, a traditional milk and ginger tea hosts serve their guests.

Rwanda isn't what most people think of when they think of a holiday destination, but Rwanda's capital, Kigali, is one of the fastest-growing regions in Africa and has ambitions to become one of Africa's most innovative cities. In recent years it has even been gaining a name for itself as the home city of a rapidly expanding tech industry—finding a "Made in Rwanda" tag on a laptop is difficult now, but that might be changing soon.

Another source of innovation in Rwanda is the traditional art known as *imigongo*. Nominally the activity of Rwandan women, imigongo is an intricate art form made by patterning and molding cow dung for decorating plates, panels, and wall hangings. Imigongo is said to have existed as a form of wall decoration since the eighteenth century, but the art form nearly died out with the Rwandan genocide in 1994. Eight women survivors carried imigongo forward following the tragedy, and now the art survives in the Kakira Imigongo Collective, a workshop open to tourists.

The cow isn't an arbitrary celebrant. Rather, cows in Rwanda are considered status symbols, sort of like nice cars but with a far greater cultural value. Take the customs of the traditional Rwandan wedding. Rwandan celebrations are many and carried out with gusto (birthday boys and girls have water dumped on them for good luck), but none match entertainment and ceremony quite like the wedding. This three-part affair begins with a traditional chapel ceremony, followed by a "cow ceremony" in which the requisite bovine dowry is handed over to the family of the bride, after which the groom's family acts out a drama for the entertainment of the newlyweds and their guests. The whole party wraps up finally at the local courthouse, where both the happy couple and the transferred cattle are accounted for.

66

PERSIAN

(Farsi)

وش
ب هسالمتی
(noosh),
(bee salaama'tay)

("Drink," "To health")

می نوش که عمر جاودانی این است
[*mei noosh ke om're jov-dani in ast*]

خود حاصلت از دور جوانی این است
[*khod haselat az dow're ja'va'ni in ast*]

هنگام گل و باده و یاران سرمست
[*hengom-e gol-o bode-o yaran sar'mast*]

خوش باش دمی که زندگانی این است
[*khosh bosh da'mi ke zen'de'goni in ast*]

Drink wine, for this is life eternal.
This is all that youth will give you.
It is the season for wine, roses and drunken
    friends.
Be happy for this moment, this moment
    is your life.

—Omar Khayyam

281

Persian over the past three thousand years is comparable to French in the nineteenth and twentieth centuries: both highly prestigious languages with huge followings, both Indo-European (Persian is not directly related to Arabic), and both their cultures have been and often still are associated with riches and fine living. They've each got a huge literature and famous poets who rhapsodize on the virtues and vices of wine, and both of them have got pockets of speakers that surge well and far beyond the borders you might expect: scoop your hand in the Persian language stew, and you'll come up with speakers as far away as Malaysia and North America.

Like a secret agent, Persian juggles a few names—Farsi (from Arabic *parsi*, or Persian), Dari and Pashto (in Afghanistan), and Tajik (in Tajikistan). The Galle Trilingual Stele, which contains inscriptions in Chinese, Tamil, and Persian, was erected in Sri Lanka in 1409 by the Chinese explorer Zheng He, and serves as a poignant reminder of just how ubiquitous the language was. This is not the situation now—although Persian speakers in Iran, Afghanistan, Tajikistan, and elsewhere may number as high as 62 million first language speakers and 110 million second—but it's helpful to keep in mind some idea of Persia's enormous influence.

During the reign of the medieval Seljuk Turkic empire, Persian moved fluidly throughout the Middle East and into Central Asia, spreading and sharing vocabulary with early Turkish, later the foundation of Azeri,

TASTING NOTE
Alcohol is forbidden in Iran; *majoon* banana and date smoothie, black tea with rose petals and sugar.

Turkmen, and modern Turkish. Roughly around the time that the Seljuks began to disintegrate (completely by the year 1200), Persian found new sponsorship with the Delhi sultanate in India and later with the Mughal Empire. Persian would serve as an official language in India right up until British colonizers replaced it with English in 1835. Its influence on Indian languages is uncontested, and large amounts of Persian vocabulary can still be found in Urdu, Bengali, Hindi, and others.

Even in English we can hardly escape the influence of Persian. Words like *caravan*, *pajama*, *shah*, and *serendipity* are all suitably foreign looking that we don't bat an eye when we learn their origin. The Persian roots of *seersucker*, *checkmate*, and *chess* may come as a surprise, as will Taj Mahal—a Persian word meaning "best of buildings." A sentence like "The scarlet rose at the bronze kiosk smells like lemons and sherry" is Persian in everything except verb and auxiliaries ("smell" is good, old-fashioned Old English), but the phrase "sugar candy" is 100 percent Persian. Shiraz by the way is a Persian city, even though the wine by the same name comes from Australia.

Modern Iran (meaning "Persia" in that language) doesn't view drinking in quite the same way as its forebearers did a millennium ago. Sharia law prohibits drinking, meaning the majority of imbibing takes place behind locked doors, in a spirit of mild and shared guilt. *Bee saloma'tee* (good health) is the same in Persian no matter which country you go to. There is also the word *noosh*, "drink," from the phrase *noosh besalamati*—"drink to health." If "nooshed," your response will then be *noosh ay joon*. Those who are able to travel through Iran are more likely to be treated to a cup of brown tea, brewed with a handful of rose petals, rather than alcohol.

Iranians take particular pride in honoring their guests, abiding by a social law—*taarof*—by which the host is obliged to offer the guest anything he or she wants, even up to ten times if the host thinks his guest has refused merely out of courtesy (although generally someone gives in before ten refusals). "Tarrofing" can be dangerous for newcomers—if a taxi driver waves aside your fee, you can be certain he is tarrofing you, and the proper etiquette on your part will be to insist repeatedly he accept the money.

Nothing particular is said when drinking tea, but when drinking water or when sharing food, Iranians will exclaim *befarmaye'ed*, meaning something like "here you are," before offering the cup or plate to a companion.

67

SOMALI

"Caafimaad ku cab" *(kafimad koo kab)*

("Drink healthily")

The dromedary camel—the one-hump camel found through-out northern Africa—takes its name from the ancient Greek word *dromas,* meaning "run-ner." Running isn't one of the first things we think of when we think of camels, but it is one of the camel's specialties.

TASTING NOTE
Alcohol is
banned in
Somalia;
mɪrra bitter
coffee,
camel milk.

A trained racing camel can clock in as fast as 40 mph in short sprints and sustain speeds of 25 mph for longer periods. Just for comparison, a top racing horse maxes out at about 55 mph.

In Somalia, where the dromedary was first domesticated around 900 BC, camels play a much more important role than that of a racing vehicle. In fact, dromedaries have been at the center of Somali life for most of its history, and to this day 65 percent of the population makes its living from the camel industry, whether as pastoralists (camel herders) or salesmen. Those numbers are diminishing as pastoralism comes under threat from an unstable government and gradual urbanization, but shepherding is still seen as the foundation of a prosperous and fulfilling life, with the camel considered the representative of everything one should be: resilient, tough, hardworking, and, more than anything, a survivor.

It's no surprise then that camels are also at the heart of Somalia's long tradition of oral poetry, an art form that has united this fractured country for centuries. "You're, my camel dear / the highest price / able to procure for me / the costliest ideal woman / that many men desire," sings a poet about to give his camel as bride price for his new wife (Cali Abokor, 40). Comparison with a camel is actually quite the compliment; a woman's elegance can even be likened to a camel walking through the sands of the desert.

The relationship between man and camel is one of the few safe, nonthreatening relationships desert-wandering Somalis have. In this land torn apart by nineteenth-century colonialism, twentieth-century Italian fascism, civil war, and warring states, hospitality and trust among strangers is rare even though most Somalis share a common religion (Islam), common language, and common ancestry. Camels unite Somalis through shared tradition, through a shared occupation, and through the sharing of camel milk—considered to be the crème de la crème of delicacies. For comparison, camel milk is always served to honored guests, while cow or goat milk is considered a last-resort beverage. Milk might be shared in an *aagaan*, a vessel passed from person to person, and someone might pronounce *caafimaad ku cab*, meaning "drink healthily," before you take a sip.

68

SWAHILI

"Ishi vizuri"
(eeshi vizuree)

("Live well")

We give names because of their sound, history, and prestige. Many common English names have a relatively arbitrary historical link, but on the other end of the spectrum, you get China, which names by logic. For example, knowing *nan* is "south" you get Hunan (lake south), Hainan (sea south), Henan (river south), Yunnan (cloud south), and so on.

Swahili is a little like this—the word *Swahili* means "on the coasts" in Arabic, and it is on the eastern coasts of Kenya, Tanzania, Mozambique, and Zanzibar that the language was originally spoken before being driven into Uganda and Rwanda by traders, Christian missionaries, and European colonists.

If you've ever seen *The Lion King*, you already know some Swahili even if you don't realize it. *Simba* is Swahili for "lion," *rafiki* "friend," and *pumbaa* "slow-witted." The names of the hyenas Shenzi and Banzai mean "savage" and "skulk," and *hakuna mattata*, as everyone knows, means "no worries." As with other Bantu languages (such as Zulu and Xhosa), Swahili is a heck of a lot of fun when you get a handle on the grammar. "The two men read two books" is pretty humdrum in English, but in Swahili, the phrase turns into this musical lip patter "Watu wawili husoma vitabu viwili." You like that alliteration? This is the bizarre and wonderful world of Swahili prefixes, where what words mean affect how they sound.

Imagine how much sense it would make if in English, words with similar meanings were spelled similarly. Say that you're reading a story where something called a *gupupaga* takes a bite out of a *gupugawa* and describes the flavor as juicy but with a squirmy texture. Reading this in English, we can make assumptions about what these things are, but we won't know for certain without recourse to a dictionary or to a gupupaga/gupugawa expert. In Swahili, complementary prefixes mean that the nouns belong to the same semantical group—these include classes like vitals (fruits, trees), augmentatives (large concepts), and diminutives (small things). For example: in the "big concepts" class, words like "love," "friendship," and "hospitality" all begin with *u*: *upendo*, *urafiki*, *ukarimu*. Linguistics terms this classification "grammatical gender." The phenomenon is common but largely arbitrary in Indo-European languages—anyone who has ever split their head wondering why German *Mädchen* (little girl) falls into the neuter gender *das* rather than feminine *die* already understands something of the nature of gender. But back to our example, if *gupu* is our prefix for a noun class of say, insects, voila: we've got something like a ladybug snacking on a mite, or a praying mantis with a beetle.

TASTING NOTE dawa vodka cocktail; Tusker, White Cap, and pilsner/lager beers; Kenya cane white rum; tea with sugar.

As we're on the topic of words, meanings, and bugs, this seems like a good time to talk about East Africa's cure-all cocktail: the dawa. This juicy concoction is brewed with vodka, Kenyan honey, lime, and crushed ice, served at happy hour, and pairs perfectly with an African sunset. Furthermore, the word *dawa* translates into "medicine" or "magic potion," and there's the idea—dating back to nineteenth-century colonial Britain—that a cocktail, specifically a gin and tonic, could prevent malaria. If that's true, our Swahili toast couldn't be more appropriate: *ishi vizuri* means "live well."

"À votre santé"
(a votrah sahn'tay)

("To your health")

Since the first MTV Europe Music Award show in 1994, there has been exactly one song winner that was not sung exclusively in English. This was "7 Seconds," a collaboration between Neneh Cherry and Youssou N'dour, probably the most famous African artist of the past thirty years.

69

WOLOF

N'dour begins the song with a passage in Wolof, passes the next verse—in English—on to Cherry, joins her for the hook, switches to French, and then goes back to English. If you were to add a verse in Arabic to the beginning and then switch the positions of French and English, you'd get a rough idea of Senegal's linguistic history over the past millennium.

Islamization began in West Africa in the eleventh century and successfully imported Arabic throughout the northwest through a dialect later known as Maghrebi Arabic, or Western Arabic. The influence of Arabic wasn't as strong in Senegal as it was farther north, and between 1150 and 1350, members of the Jolof Empire were speaking in an African language named after themselves: Jolof, or Wolof. This became the lingua franca not just in Senegal but also in Mauritania (to the north) and in The Gambia (to the south) until the time of French colonial power in the eighteenth century and the full-scale exportation of slaves. Slaves leaving from West Africa would be contained in the House of Slaves, on the island of Gorée outside the capital, Dakar, and shipped to the southeast United States and locations in the Caribbean.

The influence of Wolof-speaking slaves can be measured by some of the loanwords. They figure most prominently in the New Orleans jazz slang of the early to mid-twentieth century. Words like "jive," "dig," "hip," and "juke" (jukebox) all derive from Wolof. There are also the words "banana" and "yummy," which may or may not have their origins in Senegal. Senegal achieved its independence in 1960, but like so many other former French colonies, much of its language, culture, and education remains Francophone. Whether the trend will remain in the future remains to be seen.

An Islam-dominated country, the Senegalese are largely nondrinkers. Juice is the preferred thirst quencher, and with as many varieties as there are, it's no wonder why. You can find *jus de bouy* (sweet juice), *jus de bissap* (hibiscus), *jus de ditakh* (the juice of a kind of green fruit), *jus de maad* (a tangy concoction with sugar, salt, and red pepper), and others with guava, apple, and orange.

To toast, Wolof speakers use the French *à votre santé* (to your health), but for more special occasions, you can use a Wolof-language blessing, such as *yalla nala yalla sameu*, "may God protect you."

As with other African countries, you can't go far in Senegal without finding an excuse to dance. Here, the dance is called *sabar* and is performed in the middle of a giant circle of traditional drummers. Sabar gives participants the chance to groove like they've never grooved before, but there's a spiritual dimension as well. Every drum beat and every rhythm has its own names, and the effect of witnessing and dancing a sabar is to unite everyone in a common rhythm.

70

XHOSA

"Camagu"
(tsa'ma'goo)

("Be honored")

Foreign languages showing
up in American movies are like
naughty uncles showing up at
weddings. You don't really expect them, and once they're
there, you're constantly
worried they're going to
end up making a total
mess of things.

That's the case most of the time, from Sasha Baren Cohen's "Kazakh" in *Borat* to Amy Adams's "Mandarin," in the film *Arrival*.

So what does it look like when movies do languages right? Now you're in the territory of *Inglorious Basterds* or, more recently, *Black Panther*. Not only do actors speak a foreign language and speak it well, but the language is itself hardly well known outside of Africa. That language is Xhosa—spoken in South Africa and Zimbabwe—and sometimes known as the "click-click language" for three obvious reasons: the "c," "x," and "q" sounds.

"C" is a tisk, with the tongue behind the front upper teeth. "X" is the wide-lipped click you might use to summon a horse, and "Q" is the firm "tock" your tongue makes when it flips up against your hard palate. So the word *Xhosa* is pronounced "[*click*]hosa," Saturday is "Mg[*tock + i*]belo," and our toast is *camagu*, [*tisk + a*]magu." Pretty manageable. Get this right and you can go to something a little more difficult, like "Ndifuna ukuqala ndiqiniseka ukuba uyindod" (I want to make sure that you are a man). That would be "Ndee'funa ookoo[tock + a]la ndee[tock + i]iniseka ookooba ooyindod." Nothing to it. For real click lovers, check out Miriam Makeba singing the "Click Song," and prepare to be dazzled. Now, once you've gotten your clicks down, you're all set to have a real African experience.

Xhosa-speaking tribes are primarily in eastern South Africa, Lesotho, Swaziland, and Zimbabwe, and if you make friends with one, they may invite you to go out on the town and *masinwabe*, or "have a good time." That, or you'll be invited out for a drinking soiree. In the city, this is a regular sit-in with a good lager, but in the village the event will be presided over by a

bowl of maize beer, called *umqombothi*. Along with your companions, you sit down in a circle and pass the beer bowl—*isika*—from person to person, drinking as you go. Fair warning: you may want to inquire what's in the brew before you take a swig. Some brews have been known to contain battery acid or worse, to give the drink a little more harrumph.

Once you've gone around in the circle, you'll then want to thank your hosts for your invitation, and to do this simply and respectfully, you needn't do any more than stand up and say *enkosi ngondi mema*, or "thanks for my invitation." When addressing elders, be sure to do so respectfully with *molo-tata* for men and *molo-mama* for women. Finally, *camanga* doesn't correspond directly to our "cheers." The word is used as an offering of praise to elders and should be used respectfully.

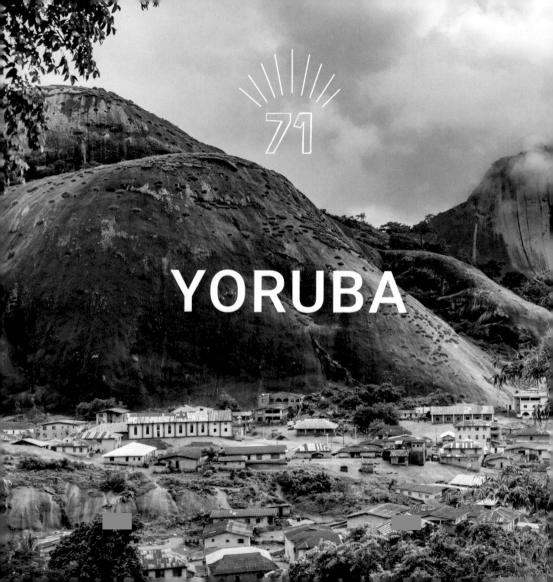

71

YORUBA

"Músò"
(moo'so)

("Cheers")

In the Yoruba creation myth,
Obatala creates land from a
shell full of sand and humans from clay. Tired
and bored, he then
takes the fruit of
a palm tree,
makes wine,
and gets
himself
drunk.

Afterward, his creations begin to show problems and disabilities, but Obatala keeps creating until eventually he passes out. The work of creation is summarily passed along to or seized by his sibling Odudawa, which ignites a rivalry that leads to the first unification of Ife, present-day Yorubaland in southwestern Nigeria.

Like Obatala sucking on palm sap on the top of the tree, Yoruba culture is steeped in the palm from head to toes. Palm oil and palm wine have an extremely important culinary function. In addition, there are palm kernels as an important source for extracting oil and for trade, palm-nut shells polished into beads for jewelry, palm fronds used for thatching, and, of course, the palm fruit itself. There are palm myths and legends and palm riddles, such as this one: "A je leran je eran a kan egungun, a je egungun je egungun a tun kan eran" (A piece of meat has an outer layer of flesh, a middle layer of bone, and an inner layer of flesh).

The answer is of course the palm fruit, which has a soft, edible outer fruit, hard inner shell, and soft interior. It ought to be obvious by now that this isn't the coconut—probably what most of us think of when we think of palm fruit—but the red palm fruit, a blood-orange-colored fruit that looks like a fat red pepper. Palm oil and palm wine are also used in treatments for patients suffering miscarriages, malaria, and smallpox, and you can even find palm oil and palm wine being used in Yoruba rituals as a sacrifice to one's ancestors.

Palm wine also lubricates the altars of Yoruban deities, called Orishas, who play a role in traditional Yoruba spiritualism akin to that of the Greek or Hindu pantheon. *Músò* is appropriate as a toast for all occasions: solemn and spiritual or recreational and rousing. And drinking occupies an important role in spiritual gatherings. Here, for rituals, prayers, or any spiritual function, the eldest member of the community will perform the ritual by first pouring out some fluid from the *ọtí ìbílẹ̀*—meaning "local drink"—and then commence with a prayer. A few other phrases are also thrown around, such as *ayo ni o* (be happy) and *kara o le* (something like "good health"). They require no drinking and can be used for any festivity you prefer.

TASTING NOTE
palm wine, kunu millet beverage, *zobo* hibiscus juice.

PART FIVE

ANCIENT, CONSTRUCTED, AND MISCELLANEOUS

72

AMERICAN SIGN LANGUAGE
(ASL)

There are between 250,000 and 500,000 speakers of ASL in the United States. That's an accurate gauge for the language itself, but it doesn't tell the full story of all the signing going on around us. Just consider how much an artfully raised eyebrow can articulate—surprise, dismay, shock, amusement, confusion, and so on.

And that's just one brow. Add a pursed set of lips, some flaring nostrils, squinting eyes, or furrowed forehead, and the tones of your expression increase exponentially. American Sign Language systematizes these expressions into a cohesive set of linguistic rules. For example, you lower your brow when asking any question that can't be answered with a simple yes or no.

How about signs in the hearing community? There are quite a few more than you might initially expect. Just take a look at professional sports: the raised finger for out balls in tennis, the bracket arms for touchdown in football, the hand T for time out, and the trio of strike, ball, and out in baseball—the contribution of the legendary deaf baseball player William Hoy. To say nothing of the various signals used in driving or cycling or scuba diving.

ASL is a little like Wi-Fi: everybody knows what it is, but no one really knows how it works. Do sign languages have grammar? (Yes.) Inflection? (Sometimes.) Can you sign complex things? (Yes.) Aren't signs just gestures for things? (No.) Is sign language international? (Good Lord, no.) Sign languages function just as regular languages, and they have their dialects, their speakers, and plenty of slang. Signs can resemble the things they are—an obvious example is our "cheers," made with two hands shaped like glasses and with a wide smile—but many signs function as complex metaphors and bear positively no resemblance to the things they are. The word for "president" is made by putting both hands on the side of your head as if outlining the brim of a tricornered hat—a sign that dates back a couple hundred years when an American president and his big hat visited a school for the deaf. Another example is the sign for "anthropology." For complex and technical terms, the modus operandi is generally to just spell the word out with your fingers, but anthropology has its own sign—one that closely resembles the sign for "I don't know."

As for an international sign standard, good luck. Sign languages are notorious loners and cross-breeders. American Sign Language and British Sign Language (BSL) arose independently of each other and belong to two entirely separate families; however, Northern Irish is mutually intelligible with ASL. Chinese Sign Language is unrelated to the Hong Kong language and shares some commonalities with BSL, including a raised pinkie to express "I don't know." Malaysian Sign Language and ASL both belong in the French sign family.

Is it proper to still say "speakers" when there's no sound? Why not? The word "speak" has roots in words meaning "to explain," "to report," or, even, "to meet" or "to assemble." It's not sound that makes the language; it's the community.

"Προς το καλον"
(pros to kal'on)

("Let's drink to all things good")

pergraecari (Latin):
"to Greek off," "to have a good time"

312

73

ANCIENT GREEK

Most of what we think about when we think about ancient Greece—politics, poetry, philosophy, theater, history, or war—comes from a small window of time between the sixth and fourth centuries BC, during the transition from the Greek polis to the Hellenistic period. Just to get things straight, there was no single ancient Greek kingdom but rather many prosperous city-states, or *poleis*, such as Athens, Corinth, Thebes, and Sparta. Greek as a mentality beyond the immediate Mediterranean collection of islands wouldn't spread until the time of Alexander the Great in the fourth century BC.

Before that, each polis had its own separate social identity. Athens was the hub of civilization; Corinth, a cradle of luxury regularly exporting some of the most well-known Greek pottery while entertaining an infamous culture of temple prostitution. Thebes was one of the first fortified Greek poleis, referred to by Homer as "Seven-Gated Thebes." Lacedaemon (Sparta) was renowned for its hoplite warriors who fought and won against the Persians in the Graeco-Persian Wars of 492 to 449 BC and then, just twenty years later, against Athens in the Peloponnesian War of 431 to 404. After winning that, Sparta became the leading power in Greece. For better or worse, Sparta's culture of war took prominence over Athens's culture of civilization, and Greece was involved in a continuous series of conflicts until its subjugation to Rome, from the second century to 31 BC.

War in the fourth century took the form of heckling the Achaemenid Persian Empire, and no one did this better than the young upstart general Alexander. Although tutored by Aristotle, Alexander was a much

315

more successful general than he was a scholar. His decade-long conquest carried him 11,000 miles from the Balkans to far western Greece, north to the Danube, south into Egypt, and east into Indian Punjab. The territory he conquered, intentionally or accidentally, occupies much of modern Turkey, Syria, Israel, Egypt, Jordan, Iraq, Kuwait, Armenia, Afghanistan, and Pakistan. However, either from severe alcoholism or assassination, not long after his foray into India in 327 BC, Alexander dropped dead, and the empire was up for grabs.

The many claimants to the crown plundered, fought, and divided the empire for over a century, during which time the Roman Empire heckled, taxed, and eventually subsumed the war-weary dynasties. Ptolemaic Egypt managed to hold off Roman conquest the longest, but in the year 30 BC, it too was consumed, kicking and screaming, by the Roman superpower. Alexander himself would have been pleased with its last queen. Beautiful, liberally educated (her languages included Hebrew, Ethiopian, Arabic, Syriac, Parthian, Beja, and probably Greek), and with a flair for dramatic tragedy (killing herself with an asp), Cleopatra was the perfect prima donna to sing the swan song of the Hellenism Alexander had grandly ushered in.

Although the empire hadn't lasted very long, Greek culture exercised an enormous influence over the ancient world. It had billed itself as sexy, smart, and fun loving, and this attitude toward Greekness would persist right up to the present day. The language continues to entice new learners every year, and a well-tested method to annoy classicists is to claim that Latin is the superior dead tongue.

Like English now, Greek then was the vehicle of culture and prestige, but what exactly we mean when we call it "ancient Greek" is troublesome. As things stood, there were probably as many dialects of Greek as there are islands in the Mediterranean. The dialect known as Mycenean is the earliest form of Greek known to scholars, spoken and written from around the sixteenth to twelfth centuries BC, before the takeover of four other dialect families: Arcado-Cypriot, Ionic, Aeolic, and Doric.

A combination of these makes up the Greek of Homer and Hesiod, but not the Greek of Plato, Aeschylus, or the New Testament. These works had to wait until the Greek of sixth- to third-century Athens, called Attic, Koine (common), or biblical Greek due to its use by the early apostles. It was this Greek, hammered out in the Athenian symposiums, the theaters, and the courts, that Alexander used to buttress his empire and that lasted through the Roman and Byzantine Empires to become the basis for much of modern Greek.

The Greek idea of pleasure in the form of wine drinking combined with intellectual pursuits is very much the province of Koine, and it is thus appropriate that this is the form from which we take our toast: προς το καλον, meaning "to the good," in the sense of "let's drink to all things good."

74

ARAMAIC

(Syriac)

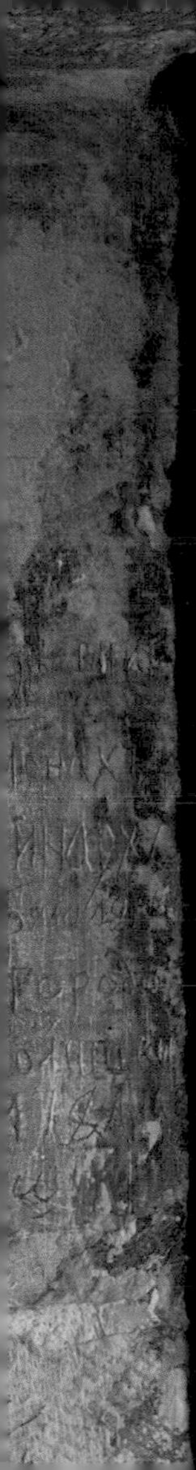

"ᴎᴀᴐᴋ"

(hub'bow)

("Love")

If you were planning a trading
voyage to Asia in the late fifteenth century, what kind
of interpreter would you
bring with you? Consid-
ering the number of
medieval Arab traders
along the spice route,
Arabic would be a
good choice. This
is precisely what
Columbus decided
when he embarked
on his trip to the
New World.

319

His translator, Luis de Torres, a Jewish convert to Catholicism and the first Jew to set foot in the New World, knew some Arabic and Hebrew, as well as Portuguese. So far, all of these are logical enough—Columbus was probably expecting to run into some Jewish traders on his route—but de Torres also spoke Aramaic, which was about as old-fashioned then as it is now. (It goes without saying that de Torres's languages turned out to be all equally useless.)

It's strange to think of Aramaic as a world power, but its position on the world stage during the millennia from approximately 600 BC to AD 600 was as powerful as that of the Arabic that replaced it. This is all the more exceptional considering that Aramaic's big break wasn't the result of widespread conquering, like Greek or Arabic, but from political endorsement. This was by none other than Darius the Great, the leader of the Persian Achaemenid Empire in the sixth century BC.

Darius was famous enough in his own time to make a pretty good name for himself as a protector of the Jews in the Old Testament, but now many know him as the Persian emperor who lost to the Greeks at the Battle of Marathon. When Darius inherited the kingdom, he was left with the problem of what to choose for a national language. A Persian dialect would have seemed like a natural course of action, but there were a number of factors involved. The languages of his legendary predecessor Cyrus (also the Great), Middle Elamite, was on its way out, and the courtly Persian was a language of prestige, unsuitable to be accorded status as the common language. Akkadian, spoken by many of the

Babylonian migrants he'd just inherited, would have been a suitable choice, as was Lydian, the language of Anatolia (Turkey). But the decision was ultimately Aramaic, which like Hebrew and Akkadian, was then the language of a displaced people—the Aramaeans of northern Syria. Aramaic's rise to fame was the language equivalent of a full-scale Oprah endorsement. Its status changed overnight from the tongue of the wandering homeless to a language with imperial prestige. Within a short time, Aramaic marginalized Akkadian and pushed Hebrew into a strictly liturgical frame.

TASTING NOTE
arak liquor,
mate tea
beverage,
muggeli
spice tea.

A huge part of this quick takeover was due to Aramaic's technical superiority. Unprecedented in its day, it was one of the first languages in the world to use a phonetic alphabet. Before this, imperial statements and literature had to be written out using a laborious cuneiform alphabet of complex logograms, like modern Chinese. This alphabet wasn't Aramaic's idea but rather something picked up from the Phoenician traders doing business in the Mediterranean. Unfortunately, samples of Phoenician writing are in seriously short supply, but Aramaic is well documented because of the Achaemenid paper empire, and by paper, I mean stone.

In terms of the language spread and history of the Mediterranean empire, you can tell the story with four languages. The first is Akkadian, a powerful judiciary language that existed as early as 2800 BC and lasted until the turn of the first millennium. Enjoying its thrust from Achaemenid Persia, Aramaic (number two) was already taking the reins a few centuries before the demise of Akkadian. It rose alongside the Greek (three) of Alexander the Great; however, the policy of the two languages was not every man for himself but of mutually exclusive divide and conquer—Greek in the East, Aramaic in the West. Aramaic did fairly well until around the second century AD; Greek, until the sixth century. Both were eventually swept aside by Arabic (four), which emerged as the supreme and total victor of the Middle East, then as it is today.

Akkadian has long since departed into the realms of classical scholarship, but most of the other displaced languages are still around. Hebrew, pushed this way and that for millennia and confined for long years to the Jewish liturgy, only reemerged as a spoken language in Israel at the end of the nineteenth century, albeit radically altered. Egyptian retreated into the worship of the Christian Church and became modern Coptic, and the descendants of Aramaic (which resemble ancient and biblical Aramaic about as well as ancient Hebrew does modern, or Anglo-Saxon does modern English) survive in a few dialect families with speakers scattered across Iraq, Iran, Turkey, and Syria.

While there are a couple modern descendants of Aramaic (termed Neo-Aramaic) with upwards of 500,000 to a million speakers, the descendants of the literary Middle Aramaic, which emerged in the first century AD, have not been so fortunate. Outside Syriac and Chaldean churches, the last remnant of the language that once dominated the

Middle East has all but faded. It's predicted the language may give way to final silence in as little as a decade.

Before that time, however, those who wish to hear this ancient tongue in all its glory can find it not spoken but sung in the verses of Father Seraphim, a Georgian Assyrian Christian who chants biblical psalms in this two-thousand-year-old language. Witness the awesome power of the chants and take this Syriac toast, which translates into "love." Something all Syrians could use now.

"Ja vie sano"
(ja vee sa'no)

("To your health")

In researching this chapter,
I came across the following
exchange in the comments
under an Esperanto-language
YouTube video:

Speaker A: Has Esperanto failed to
become the universal language?

Speaker B: Of course not! It just
hasn't succeeded yet.

75

ESPERANTO

If you can find anything more Esperanto than hopeful Esperantists (or "hopeful hopefuls") waxing positive on the future of their language, I'll buy you a beer at the next World Esperanto Congress. Actually, I believe there is such a thing: hopeful Esperantists *singing* about other hopeful Esperantists who feel ostracized by the world until they . . . meet at an Esperanto congress (see the Esperanto language song: "Sola").

Let's take a quick step back. Esperanto is the brainchild of conlanger Ludwik Zamenhof, who first published the book *Unua Libro* in 1887 under the name Dr. Esperanto—"hopeful." The book might have been small, but these hopes sure weren't. Zamenhof had set out to construct an easy-to-learn language that could unite the world and serve as an international standard, bringing speakers of entirely disparate linguistic or cultural communities under a shared, green star. Zamenhof wasn't the first to design a language with the goal of uniting the world—the unfortunately named Volapük language had its book published less than a decade before *Lingvo Internacia* and provided much of the initial audience for Esperanto—but it has been the most successful. So successful was it in its early years in fact that after the 1911 Xinhai revolution in China, there was a bid to change the national language to Esperanto. This didn't happen, but Esperanto did gain some glory in 1954 when UNESCO passed a resolution granting Esperanto support as an international auxiliary language. Language platforms like Duolingo, Lernu, iTalki, and Google Translate all have Esperanto support and services, and if you're looking for a chance to practice, there has been a world congress each year for over a century.

If all of this doesn't impress, just consider the number of speakers: at least two million, and with some numbers as high as ten (although this estimate is, well, *esperema*). Here's the real kicker though—an estimated two thousand of them are *native speakers*. If there was ever any doubt that a constructed language is no less authentic than organic languages, there's your proof. And there are other ways to gauge a language's authenticity—that is, in the culture that it inspires. J. R. R. Tolkien knew this relationship between language and culture better than any other conlanger of his or anyone else's day, and Esperantists have their own cultural quirks that aren't limited to hope-inspired sing-alongs. Generally, these quirks are inspired by the occasion of Esperanto congresses, the flavor of which is largely young, international, and with a spirit of adventure. You can find the same type in Pasporta Servo, a homestay/couch-surfing service that connects youths with hosts and encourages them to speak naught but Esperanto. Esperanto literature also has its merits, which include no less than three nominations for a Nobel Prize for Esperanto-language works (by the Scottish author William Auld). There is also Esperanto fashion (green, with green stars), Esperanto film, an Esperanto anthem, an Esperanto holiday—Zamenhof Day, December 15 (during which those most dedicated of Esperantists are encouraged to celebrate by publishing an Esperanto book)—and, naturally, an Esperanto toast: *ja vie sano* (to your health).

"סייחל סייחל"
(l'chaim l'chaim)

("To life, to life")

סעניא ויא עלא רימאל [*lomir ale in eynem*]
סעניא ויא עלא רימאל [*lomir ale in eynem*]
ווייַ עלעזעלג א ןעקנירט [*trinken a glezele vayn*]
סעניא ויא עלא רימאל [*lomir ale in eynem*]
סעניא ויא עלא רימאל [*lomir ale in eynem*]
ווייַ רעלייַרפֿ ןוא קיטסול [*lustik un freylekh zayn*]

All together
All together
Drink a glass of wine!
All together
All together
Happy and merry be!

—traditional Yiddish drinking song

328

76

HEBREW

The consensus among Polish Christians in the nineteenth century was that a Jewish drunk was hard to find. Ironically, Jews leased up to 85 percent of Polish taverns from the eighteenth to twentieth centuries, but the Jews were viewed by their non-Jewish patrons as scoundrels for letting them get drunk and waste their money. But was this sobriety true?

The tavern leasers probably had a hand in promoting the stereotype, as a sober Jewish tavern leaser painted a more respectable image than a drunk one. Yet the evidence supports the fact that abstinence wasn't common among all Jews. With the rise and spread of Hasidim in the eighteenth and nineteenth centuries, spirited worship services became the new vogue. Alcohol, especially among Jews in Eastern Europe, became a vehicle of worship and did some damage to the sober stereotype.

The Hasidic drinking philosophy was simple enough—alcohol enlivened the senses and promoted an attitude of cheerfulness appropriate to the worship of God—but there were plenty of abuses of the code, as could be expected. Nevertheless, this kind of worshipful drinking illustrates some of the key differences between the drinking then and now of Jewish societies. Getting drunk may not have been as habitual among Jews as non-Jews, but that's not to say that it didn't happen. Depending on the circumstances, drunkenness was encouraged—even required.

There is a saying: "Gentiles drink to forget; Jews drink to remember." During the festival of Purim—the holiday commemorating how the Jewish people were saved from genocide as recorded in the book of Esther—some Jewish societies are encouraged by their rabbis to become so drunk that they can't tell the difference between the phrases "cursed be Haman" (the Persian vizier who wanted the Jews killed) and "blessed be Mordecai," their savior. During Passover, four cups of wine are ritually drunk, to symbolize the four redemptive promises of God when the Jews were led out of Egypt. Finally, there is the obligation among many Jews that on Shabbat they invite someone to their home to relax and have a glass of wine.

TASTING NOTE
Tubi 60 liquor,
arak liquor,
Manischewitz
kosher wine.

The most famous wine has to be Manischewitz Concord; though it is certainly the most well-known kosher wine, it's far from being the only option. As a matter of fact, in recent times vineyards in Napa Valley and Israel have invested more and more in producing quality wines to Jewish culinary and production regulations. The day appears to be coming soon when kosher wines will no longer be associated with the taste of low-alcohol, high-sugar-content grape soda. And before you ask, yes, there are kosher spirits—quite a few of them.

What non-Jews need to know about social drinking in this culture is minimal but important. If a Jewish friend invites you into their home on Shabbat and offers you a glass of wine, accept, but refrain from touching the bottle. And as for toasting? Everybody already knows *l'chaim* (to life), but to get the proper spirit of the toast, say it twice: "L'chaim l'chaim." It's true for Hebrew as well as Hebrew's two daughters, Ladino (among Sephardic Jews) and Yiddish (Ashkenazi Jews).

77

LATIN

"Prosit"
(proseet)
("Profit")

Hedone dicit: Assibus (singulis) hic bibitur; dupundium si dederis, meliora bibes; quartum (assem) si dederis, vina Falerna bibes

For one coin you can drink wine
For two you can drink the best
For four you can drink Falernian

—inscription found in tavern in Pompeii

It's probably true that world history as we know it would appear vastly different if the Roman Empire hadn't drunk so much wine. It is certain that wine as we know it would be vastly different if there hadn't been a Roman Empire to cultivate it. Minus the obvious lack of alcohol-related words like "tavern," "inebriate," "imbibe," and "intoxicate," more to the purposes of this book, wine itself certainly wouldn't enjoy the status or range of application it has today. You find wine in religious ceremonies, in cooking, in health, in beauty products, and pretty much in every country around the world, with thirty-one billion bottles of wine sold each year. We have the Romans to thank for this.

The golden age of wine in Rome made its appearance between the second century BC and the turn of the millennium, but during its formative years, Rome was little better than sober. Tyrants couldn't offer any better than one cup of wine to satisfy Jupiter. In the second century AD, Romans received the cult of Bacchus, the god of wine, but as early as 186 the Romans had had enough of drunken immorality and went about destroying Bacchic shrines and liquidating his followers, about seven thousand in total. Tragic as the massacre was, it was all the more deplorable in that Roman policies toward the vine did a complete reversal less than forty years later.

This was due to the leveling of Carthage in the Punic Wars and the appearance of the viticulturalist's manual *De Agri Cultura*, translated into Latin and circulated among landowners. Viticulture soon became a booming industry, ruled by booming Roman boozers whose drunken antics surpassed anything modern frat houses could conceive of. A highlight reel of Rome's greatest drunken hits would include images of Marc Antony, lover of Cleopatra and doomed Roman general, sallying into his last battle dressed as Bacchus: a garb also donned by Emperor Caligula. There would also be snapshots of Emperor Nero's drunken orgy, featuring immolated Christians. Contrasted with this would be the much more liberal sip and chat known as a convivium (the same as the Greek symposium, only now with women!). Finally, there'd be a look at a Pompeeian single-room tavern—*taberna*—where there were any number of wines to wet your whistle.

TASTING NOTE
Mulsum spiced honey wine, wine with water, Falernian and Caecuban wines, anything at all . . . as long as it's not beer, unless you're a barbarian.

Indeed, wine had become so popular by the turn of the millennium that consumption had reached Hemingway danger levels: about 180 million liters of wine drunk every year, or roughly a bottle of wine per citizen, every day. The importance was in the intoxicating effects as well as in that wine rations for the army presented a nonpolluted beverage, as opposed to water.

There were also many varieties of wine. Writing around AD 60, the agriculturist Columella listed about twenty different types of grape, but Pliny the Elder in his *Natural History* writes that the varieties of wine were impossible to fathom for anybody but Democritus. If that sounds like an arbitrary judgment, consider that it was Democritus who philosophized the first atomic theory of the universe. Pliny also lauds the Roman general Cato the Elder both for his war campaigns and for his practical advice in cultivating vines.

Just a few sentences are reserved for beer, which he refers to as "grain soaked in water," drunk in the West. Indeed, beer/ale, despite large drinkers in Gaul (Germany), hardly captured Roman interest—certainly not with its associations with barbarians.

Wine was Roman, drinking was Roman, and our toasting traditions probably have a lot of Roman behind them: clinking glasses to ward off bad spirits, raising a glass to the health of a god and to the emperor, and the advent of a communal jar for pouring, for fellowship, and also because if it were poisoned, it would take everyone down with it.

Prosit, from the verb *prodesse* (to be beneficial) means simply "let's enjoy," but there are alternatives, such as *salutaria*, "to health"; *propino tibi salute*, "I drink to your health"; and *bibe multis annis*, "drink that you may live many years."

78

NA'VI

"Nitram nì'aw"
(ni'tram nee'aw)

("Happy only")

All the languages we've looked at so far share one thing in common —they are or were all spoken by humans. Which means that here, just to shake things up, we're going to take a look at something a little different: a language specifically designed to represent nonhuman speakers.

There are actually more of these floating around than people would think. Computer-programming languages, for example, are never intended for direct human communication, but by "nonhuman," you're probably thinking along the lines of alien—that is, along the lines of Klingon.

I seriously considered writing a Klingon chapter for this book. Not only is this guttural, harsh, choking, confrontational, highly developed language a heck of a lot of fun if you like cursing and seeing your spit fly ("cheers" is *iwlij jachja* [*iw lich joch jaj*], "may your blood scream"), but it's got the most dedicated language fan base of any conlang outside Esperanto, and it solves once and for all the question of whether an artificial language can have a real culture. Not to mention that Stephen Fry starred in a Klingon-language production of *Hamlet* (in which the famous line "whether 'tis nobler in the mind to suffer the slings and arrows of outrageous fortune" is deliciously rendered "quv'a', yabDaq San vaQ cha, pu' je SIQDI" [Is it honorable when, inside the mind, one endures the torpedoes and phasers of aggressive fate?]). There is also a Klingon *Christmas Carol* (featuring the likes of a dishonorable sQuja), Klingon karaoke, and a full-length Klingon opera. But that's enough about all that.

Na'vi, the language of James Cameron's *Avatar* (2009) may not yet have this much prestige right now, but it's come a long way since the release of the first movie, and it's got all the elements for success: a full-length dictionary of two thousand words, a complete grammar (designed specifically for the movie by the PhD linguist and conlanger Paul Frommer), and—that most central element of a language's survival—an active group of speakers. But how do you make a language look *alien* when the grammatical and phonetical rules have to be outfitted for a *human* speaker?

Frommer used a couple solutions. One of the more obvious features is something called ejective consonants for the letters *p* (px), *t* (tx), and *k* (kx). These are made by letting air collect in your mouth and then ejecting it with the consonant sound. It's quite a bit simpler to do than to describe. If you're waiting on an important phone call, and the call comes two hours too late, and the caller says, "Hey, sorry, I didn't have my phone on me," and you purse your lips and mutter something sarcastic to yourself along the lines of "Phh, really?" that "phh" sound isn't voiced through your throat but from the air in your mouth. Amplify, and you've got it.

Next up are the infixed conjugating verbs. Here's an example to get your infix on, using the German verb *trinken* (to drink): "I drink" is *ich trinke*; "you drink," *du trinkst*; and "he drinks," *er trinkt*. In most languages, the changes in the verb fall on the end. In Na'vi, this happens in the *middle*, meaning "I drink" becomes *ich tr(e)ink*, *du tr(st)ink*, and *he tr(t)ink*.

Thankfully, Na'vi drinking doesn't make as much of a hassle as its grammar. There are two toasts you can choose from: *nitram nì'aw*, meaning "happy only," which is a pretty good expression of "cheers," and *fpom-tokxìri niväk ko*, meaning "let's drink to health." Presumably, as the Na'vi do not use glass, there would be no clinking, yet interested learners will simply have to wait and see how the language evolves. And evolve it will. With no less than four possible sequels slated for the future, hobbyists ought to have ample time and opportunity to brush up on their Na'vi.

79

QUENYA

(Elvish)

"Almiën"
(al mee en)

("To good fortune")

So-called artlangs are those languages such as Na'vi, Dothraki, and Klingon representing a subspecies of language creation designed to fulfill an artistic or creative urge. At least, that's what some people would have us believe.

343

But hold on a minute—don't all languages respond to these needs? Wasn't the person who heard the call of the cuckoo and then proceeded to refer to the bird by that call responding to a creative urge? There's a difference between conlangs and natural languages certainly, but it's not a creative difference but rather a difference in control and a difference in how the public perceives you.

"My real subject is . . . nothing less embarrassing than the unveiling in public of a secret vice"—that's J. R. R. Tolkien delivering a lecture on the subject of his fascination with constructed languages. In 1931, Tolkien was thirty-nine and a successful Oxford teacher of medieval languages (Old English, Old Welsh, Old Irish, Gothic—evidence of how much the literature of these languages, along with Finnish, can be found in the number of poems and stories trickling out from the Tolkien estate every two years or so), and yet somehow, he's *embarrassed* by it all, rooting it in "childish make-believe." This is unbelievable in today's world, where conlanging is becoming increasingly marketable, but Tolkien is in earnest not just about his embarrassment but about his obsessive fascination. In fact, you could make a serious claim that *The Lord of the Rings* was written around a pair of constructed languages that by the book's publication had been in the works for around forty years.

TASTING NOTE
ale, mead,
Old Winyards
red wine
(hobbits, men),
Miruvor
mead-like
cordial, (elves),
grog (orks).

Now seems like a suitable time then to open a discussion on the languages of Middle Earth, for languages they are. Perhaps there are not as many as diehard Tolkien fans would attest to, but there is certainly a large group: two usable forms of Elvish (Quenya, "Elvish Latin," and Sindarin, demotic Elvish), four fragmented Elvish languages (one of which might be a primitive form of Sindarin), some fragments of two Mannish languages (of Numenor and Westron, or Common Tongue), a vocabulary and possibly more of the Dwarfish language Khuzdal, and some other miscellaneous fragments and vocabulary in about five more. He also developed an alphabet, Tengwar, for dressing up his Elvin creations.

And he also developed quite a drinking culture for his characters in *The Lord of the Rings*: ale for men and hobbits, wine for the men of Laketown and for the wood elves (who call it *míruvórë*), and ale/beer/lager/mead for the dwarves (*goraz*, *gorog*, *garan*, and *goroj*).

Unfortunately, to my knowledge, Middle Earth anthropologists have yet to extract a reliable toast from the mountains of the dwarves, but there is *menu ziramu gamildu* (you forge with the ancients), which one could very easily imagine being tossed around in the Dwarven drinking halls. Among the hospitable elves, we fair quite a bit better. In Sindarin (the Elvish of Legolas), we get *ai*, an interjection meaning "hail," and the phrase *panno i hûl nín*, or "fill my cup!" In Quenya, *ai* becomes *alar/alla*, and "fill my cup" becomes *á quanta yulmanya*. And there is even a proper cheers: *almiën* (literally "to good fortune").

But Quenya really isn't the sort of thing you'd drop into if you're enjoying a few pints at the Prancing Pony, unless you're a Baggins. (Bilbo, for the record, was a fluent speaker of both, while his nephew Frodo, schooled in Sindarin, had only a passing knowledge of Quenya.) However, should you happen to be a well-traveled hobbit who had tasted the outside, some good Sindarin encouragement would certainly be in order. Lift your pint, give a clink, and pronounce the name of your celebrated companion: "Ai, Bilbo!" or "Ai, Frodo!"

Do languages make culture? Absolutely. Even more than that, languages make friends. Sixty years after the publication of *The Lord of the Rings*, with Tolkien fandom still soaring, it's hard to argue with the man.

"Nasa pona"
(nasa pona)
("Drunk good")

There are as many reasons to
invent a language as there are
language inventors. J. R. R. Tolkien proved whole worlds could
be distilled from languages, while
Ludwik Zamenhof believed an invented language contained the elements that could unite all peoples
regardless of different linguistic
backgrounds. You've also got
your professional craftsmen
like Paul Frommer (Na'vi),
Marc Okrand (Klingon),
and David Peterson
(Dothraki).

However, here we will deal with a different type of language philosophy altogether—the idea that language can affect how you perceive the world on a grand scale.

This idea belongs to the domain of the controversial topic of linguistic relativity, or the Sapir-Whorf hypothesis, which holds that speakers with languages of different grammars are directed by their language into different observations and evaluations of the world. That seems like a no-brainer at first. Take the word "dry." In the context of Culture A, which lives in a rainforest, the word might mean "without water," while in Culture B, living in a desert, it means "strong, stable," in the sense of wet clay becoming more durable once it has dried. Notice however the use of the word "culture" instead of "language," for it is here that much of the controversy lies.

How do you separate a culture from a language? Does language influence culture? Is it the other way around? Or is the process a two-way street?

In Sonja Lang's Toki Pona, easy and fun pronunciation, simple grammar, and lack of complexity are all designed to put the speaker into a simple state of mind. Toki Pona (literally "good speech") is a minimalist construct whose focus on simplicity and positivity was designed through a process of Tokiponization to declutter your mind and get you focusing on what is most fundamental. In pursuit of simplicity, Toki Pona confines itself to a lexicon of just 123 core vocab words and a syllabary of nine consonants and five vowels (compare with twenty-four consonants and twenty vowel sounds in English). There is also no inflection, no verb conjugation, no tenses, no gender, and no plurals. There are just three numbers—1 (*wan*), 2, (*tu*), and 5 (*luka*). You can count as high as you want (luka tu tu, 5 + 2 + 2 = 9), but there's a cap at around 14 (luka luka tu tu) after which you get things like luka luka luka luka luka luka luka (35): precisely the kind of clutter Toki Pona discourages. Unless the number 35 is absolutely essential to your meaning, much better to use *mute* (many). Ditto the body, where *noka* comprises thighs, legs, and feet, and *luka*, arms and hands. As for "cheers," because we already know *pona* equals "good," stick it behind *nasa* (wild, drunk, or strange), and voila. I propose an alternative as well, *moku e pona* (*moku e*, meaning "to eat, drink, or swallow): "drink good." Easy.

So easy in fact that new speakers are actively drawn in by a kind of Toki Pona challenge—achieve fluency in two weeks, learn core vocabulary in just two hours, and so on. The language also boasts its own set of emoji-like pictographs, which may not be practical but sure are fun. And that's about all there is to it.

Whether Toki Pona will enjoy a bucolic future like Esperanto, the glowing fandom of Quenya, the dedication of Na'vi, or whether it will enjoy its time in the sun before slipping away to language heaven is anyone's guess. Toki Pona has a lot going for it, not least of which is a rapidly expanding range of speakers.

Alas, speakership is something which cannot be said for Ithkuil, a construction by the linguist John Quijada. For a Toki Ponan, Ithkuil is just about the worst possible linguistic nightmare ever devised, what with its forty-four consonants, seven tones (Chinese has four) ninety-six cases (Sanskrit's got eight), and 1,800 suffixes and verbs, which sort of resembles a custom salad restaurant—however you like it, we make it that way. But salad puts almost too nice a point on it. Seasoned Ithkuil students can spend hours or even days putting together basic words and phrases. Here's Quijida dishing out his Ithkuil recipe: "Consonantal phonology and verbal morphology of Ubykh and Abkhaz, certain Amerindian verbal moods, Niger-Kordofanian aspectual systems, Basque and Dagestanian nominal case systems, Wakashan enclitic systems, the Tzeltal and Guugu Yimidhirr positional orientation systems, the Semitic triliteral root morphology, the evidential and possessive categories of Suzette Elgin's Láadan, and the schematic word-formation principles of Wilkins' Analytic Language and Sudré's Solresol."

Sure thing. I'm with you, but filtering your thoughts through such an arduous system just doesn't feel right for "cheers." After all, it's the crispness, the spontaneity, the simplicity, the sheer joy of the word that gives language so much of its vitality. And what could be more pona than that?

LANGUAGES BY COUNTRY

Afghanistan Dari Persian, Pashtu

Albania Albanian

Algeria Arabic

American Samoa Samoan

Andorra Catalan

Angola Portuguese

Anguilla English

Antigua and Barbuda English

Argentina Spanish

Armenia Armenian

Aruba Dutch

Australia English

Austria German

Azerbaijan Azerbaijani

The Bahamas English

Bahrain Arabic, English, Farsi

Bangladesh Bengali, English

Barbados English

Belarus Belarusian, Russian

Belgium Dutch, French, German

Belize English

Benin French, Fon, Yoruba

Bermuda English

Bhutan Dzongkha, Tibetan dialects

Bolivia Spanish, Quechua, Aymara

Bosnia and Herzegovina Bosnian, Croatian, Serbian

Botswana Setswana, English

Brazil Portuguese

British Virgin Isles English

Brunei Malay

Bulgaria Bulgarian

Burkina Faso French

Burma (Myanmar) Burmese

Burundi Kirundi, French

Cambodia Khmer

Cameroon English, French, African languages

Canada English, French

Cabo Verde Portuguese

353

Cayman Islands English
Central African Republic French, Sangho
Chad French, Arabic
Chile Spanish
China Mandarin Chinese, Cantonese, regional dialects
Christmas Island English
Cocos Islands Malay
Columbia Spanish
Comoros Arabic, French
Democratic Republic of the Congo French
Cook Islands English, Maori
Costa Rica Spanish
Croatia Croatian
Cuba Spanish
Cyprus Greek
Czech Republic Czech
Cote D'Ivoire French
Denmark Danish, Faroese
Djibouti French, Arabic
Dominica English
Dominican Republic Spanish

East Timor Tetum, Portuguese
Ecuador Spanish, Amerindian Languages
Egypt Arabic
El Salvador Spanish, Nahua
Equatorial Guinea Spanish, French
Eritrea Tigrinya, Arabic
Estonia Estonian
Ethiopia Amharic, Tigrinya
Falkland Islands English
Faroe Islands Faroese, Danish
Fiji English, Fijian
Finland Finnish
France French, Breton, Basque
French Guiana French
French Polynesia French, Polynesian
Gabon French
The Gambia English
Gaza Strip Arabic, Hebrew
Georgia Georgian
Germany German
Ghana English
Greece Greek

Greenland Greenlandic, Danish
Grenada English
Guatemala Spanish, Amerindian
  languages
Guinea French
Guinea-Bissau Portuguese
Guyana English
Haiti Creole, French
Honduras Spanish
Hungary Hungarian
Iceland Icelandic
India Hindi, English, Bengali,
  Gujarati, Malayalam, Punjabi,
  Tamil, Telugu, Urdu, Sanskrit
Indonesia Bahasa Indonesian,
  Javanese
Iran Persian, Turkish dialects
Iraq Arabic, Kurdish
Ireland English, Irish
Israel Hebrew
Italy Italian
Jamaica English, Creole
Japan Japanese
Jordan Arabic

Kazakhstan Kazakh, Russian
Kenya English, Swahili
Kiribati English
North Korea Korean
South Korea Korean, English
Kosovo Albanian, Serbian
Kuwait Arabic
Kyrgyzstan Kyrgyz, Russian
Laos Lao
Latvia Latvian
Lebanon Arabic
Lesotho English, Sesotho
Liberia English, ethnic languages
Libya Arabic
Liechtenstein German
Lithuania Lithuanian
Luxembourg Luxembourgish,
  French, German
Macedonia Macedonian, Albanian
Madagascar Malagasy, French
Malawi Chichewa
Malaysia Malay, Chinese dialects,
  indigenous languages
Maldives Maldivian Dhivehi

Mali French
Malta Maltese, English
Marshall Islands Marshallese, English
Mauritania Arabic
Mauritius Creole
Mexico Spanish
Micronesia English
Moldova Moldovan Romanian, Gagauz
Monaco French
Mongolia Mongolian
Montenegro Serbian/Montenegrin
Morocco Arabic, Berber dialects
Mozambique Portuguese, Emakhuwa, indigenous languages
Myanmar Burmese
Namibia English, Afrikaans
Nauru Nauruan
Nepal Nepali, English
Netherlands Dutch, Frisian
New Zealand English, Maori
Nicaragua Spanish
Niger French, Hausa

Nigeria English, Hausa, Yoruba, Ibo, Fulani
Norway Norwegian, Sami
Oman Arabic
Pakistan Urdu, English, Punjabi
Palau Palauan, English
Panama Spanish, English
Papua New Guinea Tok Pisin, indigenous languages
Paraguay Spanish, Guarani
Peru Spanish, Quechua
Philippines Tagalog Filipino, English, Cebuano
Poland Polish
Portugal Portuguese
Qatar Arabic
Romania Romanian
Russia Russian
Rwanda Kinyarwanda, French, English
St. Kitts and Nevis English
St. Lucia English
St. Vincent and the Grenadines English

Samoa Samoan, English

San Marino Italian

Sao Tome and Principe Portuguese

Saudi Arabia Arabic

Senegal French, Wolof

Serbia Serbian

Seychelles Seselwa Creole, English, French

Sierra Leone English

Singapore Mandarin, English, Hokkien, other dialects

Slovakia Slovak

Slovenia Slovenian

Solomon Islands English, indigenous languages

Somalia Somali

South Africa Zulu, Xhosa, Afrikaans, English

South Sudan English, Arabic

Spain Castilian Spanish, Galician, Basque

Sri Lanka Sinhala, Tamil

Sudan Arabic

Suriname Dutch, Surinamese

Swaziland English, Swati

Sweden Swedish

Switzerland German, French, Italian

Syria Arabic

Taiwan Chinese, Taiwanese (Min), Hakka

Tajikistan Tajik, Russian

Tanzania Swahili, English

Thailand Thai

Togo French

Tonga Tongan, English

Trinidad and Tobago English

Tunisia Arabic, French

Turkey Turkish

Turkmenistan Turkmen, Russian

Tuvalu Tuvaluan, English

Uganda English, Niger-Congo languages

Ukraine Ukrainian, Russian

United Arabic Emirates Arabic

United Kingdom English, Welsh, Scots Gaelic

United States English, Spanish

Uruguay Spanish, Portunol, Brazilero

Uzbekistan Uzbek, Russian

Vanuatu Bislama, English pidgin, local languages

Vatican City Italian, Latin

Venezuela Spanish, indigenous languages

Vietnam Vietnamese, English

Yemen Arabic

Zambia English

Zimbabwe English, Shona, tribal dialects

BIBLIOGRAPHY

Cali Abokor, Axmed. *The Camel in Somali Oral Traditions*. Translated by Axmed Arten Xange. Uppsala, Scandinavian Institute of African Studies, 1987. A useful, if dated, exploration of the camel in Somali society.

Dickson, Paul. *Toasts*. New York: Bloomsbury USA, 2009. An excellent collection of toasts, as well as a good history of toasting in general.

Dorren, Gaston. *Lingo*. New York: Grove, 2016. Gaston's wit and the fun he has with language encouraged much of the European-language section here. He's written probably one of the most entertaining books about languages in the past ten years.

Gately, Iain. *Drink: A Cultural History of Alcohol*. New York: Avery, 2009. A beautiful and informative history on alcohol throughout the world. Many of the European texts herein owe something to this book, and my English, French, and Chinese texts owe quite a bit.

Lukacs, Paul. *Inventing Wine*. New York: W. W. Norton, 2013. A succinct and informative history.

Lyovin, Anatole V. *An Introduction to the Languages of the World*. Oxford: Oxford University Press, 1997. This thorough and encyclopedic tour of the world's languages provided indispensable technical information.

Ostler, Nicholas. *Empires of the Word*. New York: HarperCollins, 2005. A comprehensive history of languages—and a classic. Invaluable for much of this book's language history.

Okrent, Arika. *In the Land of Invented Languages*. New York: Spiegel and Grau, 2010. An interesting take on the genre of conlangs. My Esperanto and Quenya texts were inspired by Okrent's reporting.

Tolkien, J. R. R. *A Secret Vice*. New York: HarperCollins, 2016. The conlang master's own words about his craft. Interesting for Tolkien and language lovers alike.

BRANDON COOK
is a writer and language
enthusiast. He currently lives in China.
Cheers! is his first publication.